BEYOND IKENICK CREEK

TRACEY MAYFIELD

ISBN 978-1-68197-557-3 (paperback)
ISBN 978-1-68197-558-0 (digital)

Copyright © 2016 by Tracey Mayfield
All rights reserved. No part of this publication may be reproduced, distributed, or transmitted in any form or by any means, including photocopying, recording, or other electronic or mechanical methods without the prior written permission of the publisher. For permission requests, solicit the publisher via the address below.

Christian Faith Publishing, Inc.
296 Chestnut Street
Meadville, PA 16335
www.christianfaithpublishing.com

Printed in the United States of America

All characters and events in this book are fictional, and any similarities to people or situations are purely coincidental.

For those readers familiar with the McKenzie River and the surrounding area, certain details of the location depicted have been adjusted to fit the story. Ikenick Creek actually flows into Clear Lake, which is where the McKenzie River begins. Also, the time frame for medical and nursing interventions has been shortened to facilitate the development of the story. All other information has been verified by research and is correct to the best of my knowledge.

Campers

Eli—sixteen; has a juvenile record, was raised by a single mother, and had a life-changing experience as a child

Amber—sixteen; hasn't spoken in nearly a year due to depression and guilt from a tragic accident

Matt—fourteen; orphan who was raised at camp by his grandpa

Carter—thirteen; scrawny camper who is bullied at school and is afraid of everything

Zack—fourteen; overweight camper who was abandoned as a baby and raised in foster homes

Kalvin—eighteen; smooth-talking con artist and gambler

Mason—eighteen; recovering addict who had a privileged childhood with his affluent family

Bo—seventeen; has an arrest record for burglary and car theft and his girlfriend is expecting a baby

Vaughn—sixteen; has anger-management issues and an abusive father at home

Eddie—seventeen; has the IQ of a genius and used it to hack into his high school's computer system

Max—fifteen; runaway living on the streets after he refused to follow the rules at home

Derek—fifteen; instigates fights at school and at camp

Staff

Judge Mosaron—sentences troubled youth to a camp-like correctional facility

Trevor—camp director who turned his life around and wants to prevent kids from making poor choices

Junior (aka Earl)—counselor for Courage cabin who started the camp with Trevor

Gabe—main security guard at camp

Ms. Reid—teacher at camp

Officer Bradley—law enforcement officer who works with Judge Mosaron

Other Characters

Mom (aka Elizabeth), TJ (aka Timothy Joel), Aunt Bea, Charlotte (aka Charlie), Mrs. Evans, Alexis (aka Ali), doctors, nurses, additional hospital personnel, and other campers and staff

DEDICATIONS

To everyone who weathered the storms of life, flew with broken wings, and became a stronger, better person because of their journey.

To Brian, Sydney, and Isaac for their love and encouragement.

ACKNOWLEDGMENTS

Thank you to my friends, family, and the staff at Christian Faith Publishing for your support, advice, and suggestions for Beyond Ikenick Creek.

I thank God for giving me the ability to write words of hope and inspiration for others. With him, anything is possible.

I hope you enjoy my portrayal of overcoming obstacles and finding what truly matters.

CHAPTER 1

*L*ife, it's a relatively simple word—two consonants, two vowels, and one syllable. We all have one, but how we choose to live it makes us who we are. Boy or girl, rich, poor, skin color, clothes, social status—it doesn't matter. We each have the power to choose how to react to, cope with, and move beyond the challenges we face. I believe that what doesn't kill you makes you stronger. Life is a journey where what you want, how much you want it, and how hard you are willing to work to get it are the forces that drive you to overcome obstacles and shape who you become. This is my story.

My name is Eli. I could be any thirty-year-old man you meet on the street, except that I am me. I am five feet eleven with an athletic build, dark hair, tan complexion, and nice clothes. On outward appearance, I look like I've had a perfect life. My eyes tell a different story, though—

dark brown with flecks of hazel. They're like windows into the troubled soul of someone searching for their true purpose in life and then act like mirrors that reflect back the scars created by pain and sorrow. Fourteen years ago, my life came to a turning point. Had it not been for the judge sentencing me to spend a summer at a camp for misfits, my downward spiral of self-destruction would have led to my demise.

It is through faith and forgiveness that I am standing here today in the tall meadow grass speckled with wildflowers. The gentle, warm breeze and the distant song of the finches in the trees take me back to that summer so long ago.

The judge sat on his chair looking at me as if he was God himself handing down the sentences to the sinners of the world. His weathered skin and gray hair proved that he'd been doing this for ages, probably had heard every lie and excuse imaginable from kids like me. His dark robe looked like the standard outfit all judges wear, but there was something unexpected and different about this judge. He wasn't like the ones I had the displeasure of being in front of before. This one had a sparkle in his eye that almost gave me a bit of hope he wasn't going to throw the book at me.

"Son," Judge Mosaron addressed me sternly. "Your record has been getting longer by the year. Criminal mischief, assault, defacing public property, minor in possession, and burglary are just a few of your convictions. Now I hear you are skipping classes and on the verge of being expelled from school. You're on the fast track for a very hard life if you don't straighten up."

As I slouched in the courtroom chair, my lack of interest and respect were obvious. My dark hair hung over my eyes like curtains to hide the eye rolls, and my pierced lip was in a persistent snarl. The giant rip in my jeans, the wrinkled T-shirt, the impatient tapping of my foot in my worn-out shoes—all were indications that I was a rebellious sixteen-year-old who didn't care about himself, let alone anyone else.

I ignored what the judge had to say. *How much longer is this old man gonna lecture me? He's not my dad. That loser didn't care enough about anything but himself when he left Mom and me. I don't even remember what he looked like.*

I was barely five years old when he walked out the front door and never came back. I always wondered if I was partly responsible. Mom always reassured me I wasn't to blame. She said he just had itchy feet, couldn't stay in one place for too long. However, I overheard her telling Aunt Bea that he had big dreams and couldn't be tied down with a family. He always wanted to prove to himself—and others—he could be successful. Mom also mentioned he was battling with a guilty conscience, and he didn't want his past to repeat itself in his child's present or future. I'm sure it broke her heart when he left. They had been together since before high school, and he had been "the one." She never dated much after that and certainly never said another word about him. I wasn't sure if she just couldn't move on because of trust issues or if she just didn't have the time to. Maybe she still cared for him even though he left.

Poor Mom had done the best she could. She moved us to a small, rural community in Oregon's Willamette Valley not long after Dad left. She hoped to make a better life for us, but she had to work two jobs just to keep a roof over our heads and food on the table. Mom spent all day taking care of the elderly people at the local nursing facility, and then she would wait tables at the Dine and Dash Café just to make ends meet. By the time she got home at night, she was wiped out. Still, she pushed through the exhaustion to pay the bills, fold the laundry, and check my homework before falling into bed for a few hours of much needed sleep.

When I was younger, I had Aunt Bea to watch me before and after school. But after she had a stroke and died when I was eight, I no longer had anyone at home on a constant basis. With Mom at work in the evenings, I got sucked into some bad situations with the people I thought were my friends. By the time I hit sixteen, I spent more time skipping classes than attending. My friends had convinced me that school was for the nerds and wannabes. I could get by doing odd jobs, travel and see the country, do what I want when I want, and work the system to get what I need. They inducted me into their gang, made me a part of their family, and introduced me to crime, cigarettes, and alcohol. We would stay out half the night causing trouble in the nearby city. I was ready to learn about the truly dark aspects of society when the cops showed up at our local hangout and hauled us to the juvenile detention center. Apparently, someone ratted us out; we didn't know who did it.

I snapped back into the moment just in time to hear the judge say, "So I hereby sentence you, Elijah Parker, to spend the remainder of the summer at New Beginnings Camp for Troubled Youth. You will be escorted to the camp today by Officer Bradley."

"You can't do that!" I screamed at the judge. "You're ruining my life! I can't be forced to spend a whole summer with a bunch of criminals! I'm not a bad person! I don't even have anything packed!"

"Don't worry about that," he replied. "Your mother has already taken care of that for you."

I glared at her across the courtroom with rage in my eyes, suddenly realizing she was the informant. "How could you do this to me? I hate you!" I lashed out, furious that my own mother had betrayed me.

"You left me no choice. This is your last chance to change and become the man God wants you to be. Believe it or not, I do love you and want the best for you." Then, she quickly turned and left the courtroom so I wouldn't see the tears welling up in her eyes.

"Mr. Parker," the judge continued. "Not everybody gets a second chance to turn things around. I hope you use this opportunity wisely." And with that, he stood and exited the courtroom.

As Officer Bradley slipped the cold, hard cuffs around my wrists, I suddenly felt a knot in my stomach. The world as I knew it had come to an end. I was crushed. What now? There wasn't a single person I could trust, and I was failing most of my classes in school. I didn't have a clue about what the future would bring, but I was about to find out.

CHAPTER 2

The drive seemed to take an eternity as Officer Bradley navigated the curves through the Cascade Mountain Range. The roads weren't bad until we turned off Highway 126 onto the unpaved, winding roads in the Willamette National Forest. A small bridge marker indicated we just crossed Ikenick Creek.

The back of the unmarked patrol car wasn't exactly first-class accommodations. It was an uncomfortably warm mid-June day, and the little bit of airflow coming through the window next to me was barely enough to keep the nausea away. I was able to take my mind off the queasiness by watching the rays of sun filter through the canopy of the fir and cedar trees. I could tell it was getting toward late afternoon by the angle of the sun and the lengthening shadows. If I weren't so aware of where I was headed, I would think the peaceful scenery was somewhat of a comfort.

My zoned-out frame of mind was interrupted by the slowing of the car as it turned left onto an even narrower dirt road and approached an automatic iron gate with an on-duty guard. Connected to the gate was an enormous stone wall topped with surveillance cameras. I truly felt like I was headed to prison rather than a summer camp. I was a bit surprised to see such an elaborate facility out in the middle of nowhere.

Officer Bradley stopped briefly to speak with the guard before turning to me. "Well, kid. This is where we part ways. Beyond that gate is a chance to start over."

As he opened the door and helped me out, I wasn't sure if my legs would hold me up. I couldn't tell if it was hunger and fatigue or fear of the unknown that was making me so weak. Officer Bradley was tall and broad shouldered; I knew there was no way of attempting to run from my fate. As he led me to the entrance, the gate parted to allow us through. Once inside, he asked me to raise my hands. Gently, he removed the cuffs from my wrists.

"Don't bother trying to escape," he said. "This entire camp has tight security. Even if you made it past that, the frigid night temperatures, the wild animals, or the rugged terrain would get you."

After he handed me the bag containing my belongings, I took a long look at the place I would be calling home for the next few months. The narrow dirt road led onto a paved, semicircular drive. The east segment led to a massive log building that appeared to be a multipurpose hall. The west segment led to several smaller log structures that looked like cabins. Situated between these areas was a swimming pool, an amphitheater with a fire pit, a lush green lawn, a wire strung between two enormous trees, and a few horses in a corral attached to a large barn. A tall, wooden cross was positioned right in the middle of the camp.

Why is that here? This is supposed to be a camp for misfits, not Bible-thumpers.

I noticed a tall, slender man in his late fifties approaching us from the main building. He was wearing khaki pants, an olive-colored button-up shirt, and glasses that framed his hazel eyes. The gentle creases around his eyes and forehead complemented the graying hair, moustache, and short beard. His welcoming smile seemed genuine. He had a familiar stride and confidence about him that helped ease my fears.

"Hello, Elijah," he said with an outstretched hand. "Welcome to New Beginnings Camp. My name is Trevor. I'm the director of the camp, so come to me if you need anything."

"It's Eli!" I snarled at him. I just stood there, arms at my sides. I didn't care who he was. My mission was to do my time and get out.

Officer Bradley shook his hand and greeted him. "Thank you for your work here. It keeps the kids out of the judicial system and provides them with the skills and support they need to succeed."

"I only wish there was a program like this when I was a teen," replied Trevor. "It would've saved me a lot of heartbreak through the years."

Officer Bradley then turned to me and said, "I'll see you at the end of the summer. Keep out of trouble."

With a nod to Trevor, the last person I knew from the outside turned and walked back through the opening. The thud of the gate as it closed behind him sealed my fate. I was confined here for what seemed to be a lifetime. The sooner I was out of here, the sooner I could have my life back.

"Please follow me," Trevor said as he headed toward the main building.

I hesitated but then realized I didn't have any other options.

As we got closer to the building, I could hear music. Trevor climbed the steps and opened the heavy double doors. Inside, the room height soared to at least thirty feet with enormous beams lining the ceiling. There was a massive fireplace made of smooth boulders in the corner of the room. At the front was a stage where approximately forty teenagers stood facing two guitarists, a drummer, a keyboard player, and three singers. The music wasn't bad—almost a blend of indie rock and pop. The acoustics in the room were amazing. The crowd was singing along with the group, but I didn't recognize the song. It sure didn't sound like any camp songs I heard before.

These must be the other inmates. The boys and girls were all wearing similar outfits of khaki shorts or pants with olive-colored shirts and brown shoes or sandals. I felt like I had been dropped into some uppity prep school. "Great," I said sarcastically under my breath.

The room was set up for multiple functions. At the back were several cafeteria-style tables and folding chairs stored against the wall, along with chalkboards and rolling carts full of books. A large kitchen was to the left of the main room. Inside, two cooks quickly worked in unison. I could tell from the aroma wafting from the oven and the simmering pots on the stove that it was almost dinnertime.

There were three smaller rooms on the right side of the main room. Through the doorways of these smaller rooms, I could see posters on the walls containing math equations and periodic tables. *There was never any mention of summer school!*

Then, I realized that everyone had stopped singing and turned to look at me. I stuck out like a sore thumb in my grunge attire. My face was now red from anger and embarrassment.

Trevor escorted me to the front of the crowd and onto the stage.

"Everyone," he addressed the audience and the band, "this is Eli. He will be joining us for the summer. I would like you all to make him feel welcome. Show him around, and help him get settled into our routine here at New Beginnings Camp."

With that invitation, the other campers approached and introduced themselves to me. I decided to not remember any names. I wasn't going to be here long enough to care or make friends.

When the introductions were done, Trevor led me to a room at the back of the building. In the middle of the room, there was a table displaying a folded stack of clothes and shoes. Adjacent to this room was a small restroom.

A security guard with smooth, ebony skin and an athletic build waited by the table with his arms crossed. His tightly braided hair barely moved as he acknowledged me with a nod.

Trevor had me leave my bag with the guard while I went inside to change into my new clothes. It seemed odd that everything fit me perfectly. When I finished changing,

Trevor had me remove my lip piercing and even had the guard trim my hair. I was furious! There was nothing left of me! I barely recognized myself in the mirror on the wall.

Trevor and the guard then turned their attention to my bag. They verified there were no weapons or illicit items in the bag, removed a Bible Mom had packed for me from the side pocket, and locked the bag with my belongings in one of the numerous lockers along the wall of the appropriately named Transformation Room.

"This is all you'll need during your stay here," Trevor stated as he handed me the Bible.

I was so angry! They brought me to the middle of nowhere, took away everything I had, and now I had to be preached at all summer! There's no way I was going to stay for my entire sentence! I would rather live life on the run than live like that! I would just have to cooperate and bide my time until I found an opportunity to escape.

As I followed Trevor back out to the main area, I noticed the crowd had dispersed to outdoor activities. "Our campers are in various stages of their recoveries. As they progress, they're given more responsibilities and, in turn, earn more rewards," he explained. "The length of time for healing depends on a person's willingness, determination, and commitment to change. Some are here for only a few weeks or months, others are here for years. This experience can be as positive or as negative as you want to make it. You decide."

And with that, he motioned a blonde, stocky, red-cheeked teen over. "Matt, would you please take Eli to his cabin and get him settled in before dinner?" Trevor asked.

"Sure," he responded. "Come with me," he said with a twinkle in his eye as he bounded down the steps and across the property toward the cabins.

"I'll meet up with you later," Trevor called after me.

Just what I need—a BFF and a babysitter. This summer is totally gonna suck!

CHAPTER 3

As I followed Matt into the cabin, I noticed a carved plaque above the doorway—Courage.

"What's up with that?" I asked him.

"That's the name of our cabin," he replied. "The other boys' cabin is Wisdom, and the girls' cabins are Faith and Hope. The camp counselors named the cabins for the qualities it takes for a person to change their ways."

"Who said I planned on changing?" I snapped at him.

"It's your choice," Matt responded, "but sooner or later, you've got to own up to what you did."

"This is your bed and locker," he said as he pointed to an upper bunk across the room. I opened the attached locker to find several more sets of clothes like I was wearing along with a jacket, underclothes, boots, a three-ring binder, paper, and pencils. "Everything you'll need this summer is in there."

There were five sets of bunk beds and one full bed in the cabin. "The toilets and shower are in there," Matt said as he motioned his head toward a door in the corner. "That's Junior's bed. He's our counselor. A word of advice, don't underestimate him. He's got eyes in the back of his head."

At that moment, a huge, six feet five man in his midthirties opened the door and ducked as he entered. His shoulders were so broad and his biceps so big that he barely fit into his uniform. From the snake tattoo on his right forearm and the scar on his left cheek, I could tell he had been through some tough times. "Boys," he said, "it's time for supper."

"Junior, this is Eli," Matt announced.

"Welcome," Junior replied with a deep, stern voice as he extended his hand to greet me.

My steely glare and refusal to shake his hand didn't seem to affect him one bit.

"Suit yourself. By the way, newbie, meal times are 7:00 a.m., noon, and 5:00 p.m. I suggest you be on time. When the kitchen closes, you're out of luck until the next meal." Junior then turned and descended the cabin steps two at a time.

I put my Bible in my locker and followed Matt and Junior back across the property to the main building.

By the time we got back to the main building for the buffet-style meal, nearly everyone else had filled their plates and patiently waited at their cabin-assigned tables. We proceeded through the line, taking portions from the entrée, side, and dessert options. I have to admit the food smelled delicious, and my stomach was now cramping from hunger.

We made our way over to our table in the center of the room and sat down. As I picked up my fork and started stuffing the food into my mouth, I noticed several glances in my direction. I realized nobody else had eaten yet. I saw Trevor standing on the stage, waiting for everyone's attention. I slowly put my fork down and looked his way. With my attention finally achieved, Trevor bowed his head and closed his eyes. The other teens and counselors followed his lead.

"Lord," he began, "we thank you for the food you have provided to nourish our bodies. Let your word heal our hearts, minds, and souls. Help us to change to become the people you want us to be. We welcome our new campers and pray you give them peace and acceptance of the love you offer to them. Show them the way back to you. Teach them there is so much more than the dysfunction and worldly illusions they have been around. Lead them down the path of knowledge to fully understand the ultimate sacrifice you made to save them. This we ask in Jesus' name. Amen."

My mind wandered as I watched the group pray with Trevor. It had been a long time since I'd heard a prayer like that. Mom had tried to take me to church when I was younger, but I was too rebellious and resentful of anyone who tried to preach at me. I thought they were just hypocritical do-gooders. We had nothing in common. They knew nothing about me, and I didn't care about them.

As soon as the blessing was said, everyone started eating and visiting with their group. I chose to keep to myself and not get drawn into the conversations. Others, however, were talking and laughing about things they had done earlier that day. I tried not to look like I was listening as I shoveled the food into my mouth, but curiosity got the better of me. With my defense mechanisms briefly down, I actually started to pick up some of the names and stories of the other campers.

A scrawny kid with glasses was excited he had learned how to groom, saddle, and ride a horse. From the way it sounded, Carter seemed like a scaredy-cat. *What did he do to end up here? Looks like a wimp.*

Another camper, Zack, told how he swam the entire length of the pool without a lifejacket. *With as much extra padding as he has,* I silently chuckled, *it would be impossi-*

ble for him to not float! He looks totally harmless, so why is he here?

It was then I felt like someone was watching me. As I turned in my chair, I locked eyes with a girl across the room. She was beautiful—long auburn hair, ivory skin, slender frame. Her blue-green eyes though, revealed profound sadness and pain.

"Dude," Kalvin said, "don't waste your time on that chick. Amber hasn't said a word to anyone since she got here two weeks ago." With mischievous eyes and a smooth talking, easy-going nature about him, I could tell he'd been here for a while. If I needed the 411 on anything, I figured he would be the guy to ask.

When I turned to look back at the girl, she had disappeared. Dinnertime was now over, and everyone was clearing their tables and heading outside.

"Listen up, people," Junior said, "it's time for our evening chat. Grab your Bibles and meet me at our usual spot."

I followed my group back to our cabin and got my Bible out of my locker. We met Junior under a huge cedar tree at the edge of the central lawn. The cool shade from the tree was a nice contrast to the evening's hot, dry breeze. Other groups gathered nearby but were far enough away to prevent private conversations from being overheard. I could see Amber quietly sitting with the campers from Hope cabin.

With everyone sitting in a circle, Junior began, "At some point in the past, we've all either made bad choices or just needed some extra help through tough situations. I'd like everyone to introduce themselves to our newest cabin member, Eli, and explain what brought you to New Beginnings Camp. Remember that what's said here is strictly confidential. Eli, it's up to you if you want to share anything tonight. From here on though, you'll be required to participate. I'll start."

"I'm Earl, but my friends call me Junior. I was raised by my grandma. My parents were addicts. I dropped out of school at fifteen to join a gang and ended up in prison for nearly killin' a man in a bar fight. I met Trevor while we were doin' time. We both turned our lives around and got saved. I earned my GED and a college degree before I was released. That was over eight years ago, and I've been a counselor here ever since. I wanted to make a difference, didn't want kids to make the same mistakes I did."

What a bunch of crap! As if being saved was what changed him. I was never that bad of a person, and I sure didn't deserve to be stuck here!

Matt was next. "This has been my home for most of my life. After my parents and grandma died, I came here to live with my Grandpa Trevor. I have everything I need here—teachers, family, faith, and friends."

Poor kid doesn't know what he's missing!

"I'm Carter. I just turned thirteen. I got bullied a lot growing up. My mom and dad thought it would help if I came here to learn how to make friends and why people picked on me. I thought it was because I'm small for my age and wear glasses. I was wrong. I've learned that I wasn't the one with the problem. I'm not afraid of everything anymore, including horses!"

"Hey, Eli! I'm Zack. At least Carter knew his parents! I got dumped off at the local fire station when I was born. I can't remember how many foster homes I've been in over the last fourteen years. I was so happy the people here took the time to teach me how to swim! The kids at school said I was too fat and would never learn."

"What's up? Kalvin is the name and playin' is my game! I got busted for gambling at school. Would've been fine if my math teacher wouldn't have turned me in. Guess he was a bit ticked off I beat him at the numbers game and took him for five hundred dollars," he snickered. "I'd rather be here than in jail, though. Turning eighteen seems to be a game changer on your options. I've learned the hard way you have to earn what you get."

Really? Doesn't anyone have anything better than that?

Mason was next in the circle for introductions. He was a bit on the lanky and pasty side, then he explained why. "I came here after rehab. I started smoking pot at fourteen, moved onto booze and pills, and before I knew it, I was snorting drugs in the school bathroom. I had it all—rich parents, prep school, and was captain of the varsity football team. Now I'm struggling to earn my diploma and start my life over. I'm learning what's really important in life."

"I'm Bo," said the stocky, dark-haired teenager next to Mason. "I was sent here for burglary, sellin' stolen items, and takin' cars for joyrides. I just got lucky that I'm not in the State Penn like my dad. I figured I'd better change and fast. My girlfriend Jasmine is due in a few weeks, and I want to be there for her and the baby. I want to marry her and make things right. I love her. They deserve better than the person I was."

Now we're gettin' some drama! I was internally excited about other people's bad choices and consequences. *This group thing isn't as boring as I thought it would be!*

Next was Vaughn. He had a slightly crooked nose and a chipped front tooth. "I got kicked out of multiple schools for fightin'. I guess that was all I knew. I would sneak out of the house before dawn and return after dark just so I'd avoid the daily beatings from my dad. Pretty much everything set him off. At least here I've learned to control my anger and focus it on my interests. I hope to go to college in two years and learn auto mechanics."

"Hi. I'm Eddie," said the frail-looking teen with acne scars. "I am here for hacking my school's computers and causing mayhem with their programs. I changed some of my friends' grades to help them pass their junior year. I have the IQ of a genius, and I could've finished high school years ago. I didn't want people to think I was a dork for being intelligent, though. Here I have learned to utilize the gift God gave me. I tutor some of the other campers who have been struggling in school. I'm currently taking online AP classes, and I hope to go to the local university to earn a degree in software engineering."

Max was next. He seemed wise for his years as if he grew up way too soon. "When I came here, I literally had nothin'. I'd been living on the streets for two years. I ran away at thirteen, but that was only after my parents threatened to send me to military school. I didn't want to follow the rules, decided they weren't for me. I had to beg for money and food. I slept in alleys and on park benches. It was a very humbling time of my life. By the time I was ready to return home, I thought it was too late. There was a new sister and no room for me. So, I was sent here. I'm now caught up in school, and I feel a sense of belonging."

And then came my turn. As everyone waited for me to explain the reason for my sentence, only questions crept into my mind. *Why am I here and what is my story*? When you're placed on the spot like that, how do you sum up in a few sentences a lifetime of sadness and anger? So I just sat there.

After what seemed like an eternity of uncomfortable silence and expectation, Junior spoke, "Tonight is your one and only free pass, Eli. Each evening, I expect every cabin member to say somethin'. You can tell us how your day went, what you learned, how you feel. It doesn't matter. Sometimes talking out your problems is the start to fixing them. Well, our hour here is nearly up. I end our evening chats with a Bible verse. If you could please turn to the twenty-third psalm in your Bibles and read with me."

I vaguely heard what Junior said, but I sure wouldn't know where in that book to look even if I tried. I remember hearing it before, back when Mom and Aunt Bea would drag me to the local church as a kid. They said I needed to learn what being a Christian was truly about, how some guy over two thousand years ago sacrificed himself to save me and that he loved me. Seriously? The only saving I needed was to get away from the stares and whispers of the condescending churchgoers. I wasn't like them, and I didn't think I would ever be good enough for someone to want me as a Christian. So I quit going to church. Aunt Bea nearly had a fit when I told her I wouldn't go back. Her cheeks were flushed. She was short of breath from trying to talk some sense into me (not to mention the fact that she was heavy), and her floppy hat would bounce with every wave of her handheld fan. Mom didn't even try to argue with me. She was too worn out to try. She had learned to pick her battles with me, and this was one she wouldn't win.

Just as Junior and the other guys were saying "Amen," a bell started ringing in the distance to indicate our meeting time was over.

It's about time!

"I need everyone to put your Bibles back in the cabin, and meet me at the amphitheater. I'm going to start the bonfire." Junior then headed toward the main building to pick up the lighter and fire starter from the guard.

The guys tried to be nice and include me in their friendly banter as we did what Junior instructed. I ignored them. I didn't need their friendship. I didn't need anyone.

The hour spent around the bonfire was at least a little entertaining. Trevor and the band had nearly everyone singing. Not me, of course. There was a little bit of everything, not just churchy songs. Now that the darkness had settled in, I felt a little more comfortable. I watched the flames flicker in the pit, thankful nobody was trying to get me to engage in a conversation. As I looked around the group of campers from the four cabins, one face caught my attention. It was her! The light and shadows created by the bonfire danced across Amber's face, and her hair shined as the moonlight grazed it. She wasn't singing with the group either. I couldn't help but wonder why she looked so sad. I felt a weird connection to her, and I wondered if she would ever be interested in a guy like me. As if she heard my thoughts, Amber looked my way. My heart almost stopped! Was that a slight upward movement I saw at the corners of her mouth?

When the music ended, Trevor said it was time to return to our cabins for the night. Amber headed toward the Hope cabin with her counselor and group while I went to the Courage cabin with mine.

I climbed into my bunk exhausted from the first day of my summer-long sentence, still angry for being sent here and not intending to serve any longer than I had to. At least there was a bit of a distraction to help pass the time. And with that last thought, I fell into a deep sleep.

CHAPTER 4

Morning came way too early. I don't remember when—or if—I had ever been awake at 5:30 a.m. With the noise from the camp bell, the other guys in the cabin rushing to get ready for the day, and Junior yanking the covers off me, there was no way I'd be sleeping in.

"All right! I'm up!" I yelled at everyone.

"Good," replied Junior. "I expect everyone to be ready and the cabin sparkling by 6:45 a.m."

He sure wasn't kidding. Everyone knew what they were assigned to do and how long they had to do it. Every five minutes, a camper would rotate out of the shower room all dressed and ready to start his task. Those at the end of the line would start his task first.

"This is the weekly cleaning calendar," Junior said as he pointed to the calendar on the wall.

"Are you kidding me?" I couldn't believe that my name was assigned to clean the two toilets!

"Discipline and cleanliness never hurt anybody," answered Junior. "Each week, the assignment will change. As you proceed down the list and wind up at the bottom on toilet duty, you'll know that next week will be better. Newbies always start at the bottom."

"Here is a trick I learned," interjected Matt as he rushed around with the broom and dustpan. "If you get up right away and get into the stalls before anyone uses them, it's not that bad. The supplies are under the counter. That way, you'll at least get a shower before the hot water runs out."

"Great," I remarked sarcastically to Matt. *Oh crap!* I suddenly freaked out as I grabbed the rubber gloves, toilet cleaner, and brush and ran toward the stalls. Too late, Zack and Vaughn beat me to the toilets.

By the time I got my task finished, I only had a few minutes to get ready. I wasn't prepared for the cold shower and let out a howl as I jumped in. What an awful way to start the day, and it was only Monday! A fleeting thought crossed my mind that if yesterday was Sunday, then how was a judge able to send me here? Aren't the courts only open Monday through Friday?

I finished getting ready just in time. I wasn't about to miss breakfast and make my morning any worse.

Just like last night, everyone dished up their plate and went to their cabins' assigned table. Unlike before though, I waited until Trevor said the blessing before I chowed down.

After we picked up our dishes, Kalvin gave me a heads-up on what was next. "Hey, man. We only have a few minutes to get our binders, paper, and pencils from our lockers. We've got class from 8:00 to 11:45 a.m. and 1:00 to 4:00 p.m."

"Extra school and chores, this summer sucks!" I whined.

"You did the crime. Now you have to do the time. If I were you, I'd take advantage of the help that's available."

After that so-called pep talk, we got our supplies from the cabin and made it to the classroom as the bell rang.

All three classrooms were filled with kids from the cabins. It looked like they were grouped by approximate grade levels—seventh/eighth, ninth/tenth, and eleventh/twelfth. Max and Vaughn were in my class as was Amber. From the schedule posted on the front board, I realized we would be learning math, English, and writing in the morning and science, history, and economics in the afternoon.

I found an empty seat near the back of the room in hopes I could nap during class. No such luck. A stout middle-aged woman with glasses and hair pulled back into a bun approached me.

"Hello, Mr. Parker. I'm Ms. Reid, and I'll be your instructor during your stay with us. As with all of my students, I have obtained your report card from your school and know exactly what lesson you are on. Here are your textbooks and assignments. They are to be completed on time every day and left on your desk to be graded."

What a taskmaster! As soon as I can find a way, I'm outta here!

Sitting at my desk hour after hour was awful! I tried to zone out and ignore Ms. Reid, but she moved me to the front where I had to pay attention. I skipped school at home, because I figured I wouldn't ever need this useless information. *Seriously, would I ever use algebra and essay writing in the real world?*

My brain hurt by the time we were released for a lunch break. I ate my food in silence, already exhausted from the schedule we were expected to keep. It was hard to drag myself back to the classroom for more torture. Life science and historical facts were not my idea of fun. At the end of the school day I tried to make a quick escape from the classroom, but not before Ms. Reid pulled me aside for a chat.

"Mr. Parker," she began. "I know you are smarter than you let on, maybe more than you even know. Your assessment testing indicates you have a very high IQ, although your report card shows you are failing most of your classes.

Comments from your teachers state you haven't completed any of the assignments, and your attendance record is appalling. I expect that boredom and lack of motivation have contributed to your low performance level. I have assigned Eddie to tutor you three days each week until you are caught up to the rest of your class. You'll start after school today. We usually have free time on Monday, Wednesday, and Friday afternoons, but you will have to earn your activity choice like everyone else."

I rolled my eyes at her.

"We have a tough-love style of discipline here, Mr. Parker. Believe it or not, everything we have you do here is to help you become a better person. I'll see you in the morning."

"Hey, Eli," said Eddie as he walked up the front steps to meet me for our tutoring session. "Follow me."

We turned and headed across the property, past the horse corral, along a path, and down to a creek. Eddie sat on a shaded grassy spot beside a giant fir tree.

"Sit," he motioned to a spot next to him. "This is where I come to study. It's quiet, peaceful, and easier to absorb the information outside the classroom."

"So why do you care about helping me?" I sneered while sitting down.

"I genuinely want to help people earn their education rather than helping them to cheat their way through life.

Being closer in age than the teachers, I think I can relate to other campers better, present the information in a different light."

I sat there for a minute, watching the creek water trickle through a culvert in the perimeter wall and disappear. A fleeting thought of escape welled up in me, but Officer Bradley's words of warning still echoed in my mind.

We spent the next hour going over so much information. The weird part is the acronyms and memory games Eddie used to teach the concepts were working! *Doesn't matter. I could learn this stuff during the year at my own school rather than wasting my summer here!*

The ringing of the bell had us running to the cabin to put away our school supplies before dinner. We didn't want to get a lecture from Junior for being late.

I took my time to eat dinner, hoping to slow down the hands of time. I knew after dinner, I would be required to say something at our dreaded evening chat. Unfortunately, my silent wish to vanish into a parallel universe didn't happen. I followed Junior and the guys to our cabin to get our Bibles before heading out to the lawn.

"Hurry up!" they called to me as I dragged my feet. The closer we got to our spot, the more nervous I became.

CHAPTER 5

I sat in the shade of the cedar tree, listening to Junior and the campers in my cabin talk about their day and any past information they wished to share. My mind raced frantically as I tried to figure out what I was going to say.

"Eli," Junior said as my turn came up. "What would you like to share with us tonight?"

"This place sucks!" I exclaimed. "I would rather be dead than be here! At least then I'd be getting what I deserve!"

"Everyone here has felt that at one time or another," Junior reassured me. "Could you explain? Everything you say here is confidential and won't be repeated."

I thought for a minute as I looked around at the nine pairs of inquisitive young eyes focused on me. I had never spoken aloud about what I had done. I knew it was a direct cause for why my dad left, why I had made poor choices in the past. How could anyone forgive me?

"I...I was the reason my brother died!" I sputtered. "He was just a baby, and it's all my fault!"

As I flashed back to that horrible December day, it felt like it happened just yesterday. There was about six inches of new snow on the ground, so I was bundled up in my parka, snow pants, boots, and mittens. It was a few days after Christmas, and I was excited to take my new sled outside. I had even begged my parents to let me take my little brother out for a ride. They finally gave in.

Ian was a chubby little ball of energy. He had just turned three in November and kept my parents busy. His red cheeks and the twinkle in his eyes made you want to do anything to keep him happy. "Fastuh!" he would squeal as I pulled him on the sled.

"Be careful, Eli," Dad shouted from across the property. "Don't go near the pond!" He was sitting on the porch in a blanket, working on a project his boss wanted done by Monday. Mom had gone to the store to exchange some of the clothes I received as presents. I had just gone through a growth spurt, and the outfits were too small.

Back then, Dad's job paid so well Mom didn't have to work. She spent her days taking us to the park and teaching us the ABCs. The occasional trip to town was her "me time." She would walk through the stores without having to worry about which of us kids would pull things off the shelves. Poor Mom didn't know what she would soon face.

I was running as fast as my four-year-old legs would take us, then I would stop and let the sled drift in a semicircle. With such an unusual amount of snow on the ground, I didn't realize how close to the pond we were. The pond had recently frozen over, and the snowfall the previous night had completely covered the shoreline. I couldn't see our dock or slide.

Just as I was running and pulling the sled around a corner, I tripped over my own feet. I fell face first into the snow, letting go of the rope as I tried to catch myself. Without warning, the thin ice broke as Ian and the sled drifted across the snow several feet away from me. He immediately started splashing and flailing. "Eli, help! Cold!" he screamed over and over. I didn't know what to do. I had only taken a few swimming lessons at the town pool, and I sure wasn't good enough to save him.

"Dad!" I screamed as I ran toward the house. "Dad! Help Ian!"

He looked up from his work just in time to see Ian go under the surface of the pond. He threw his work proposal on the ground and ran across the field in his sweats and wool socks. He dove into the frigid water and frantically searched for my brother. On his third attempt, he came out with a limp small bundle. Ian's eyes were closed, and it looked like he was sleeping.

At that moment, Mom came driving up the lane in her silver minivan. She stopped and left her door open as she ran across the field to meet me.

"Ian...fell... in...water," I managed to relay to her in gasping phrases.

"Call 911!" Dad yelled to her as he put Ian down on the ground and started CPR on him.

Mom did as he said and ran to the house to call 911. I followed her. With terror in her voice, she told the operator what happened. She saw my dad doing his best to revive Ian. "Please hurry!" she begged as she hung up on the operator. I stood in the house and watched as she ran back across the field to Dad and Ian. She dropped to her knees in the snow beside them. I saw her bow her head and fold her hands.

It seemed like an eternity, but I'm sure it was only a few minutes before the ambulance came up the lane. Curious neighbors were not far behind.

Mrs. Evans had seen the commotion and came over to see what was going on. She entered the house and found me peeking out the window at the paramedics working on my brother.

"Jesus' angels are around them, you know," she commented to me. "No matter what happens, this wasn't your fault. It was just a terrible accident."

I looked at her then back toward Ian and my parents. I heard the *whump, whump, whump* of the blades as the air ambulance landed in our field. The paramedics had Ian on a stretcher and were running with him to get him loaded into the helicopter. I saw Mom climb in and sit on a bench while the flight nurses worked on my brother. Dad jumped into the minivan and took off at the same time as the helicopter. There wasn't enough room for both of them to ride with Ian, so Dad planned on meeting them at the children's hospital in Portland.

That was the last time I saw Ian. Mrs. Evans stayed with me all afternoon and evening. She tried to get me to talk about what happened and said I would feel better if I did. I decided if I pretended it didn't happen, then everything would be okay.

The phone rang while I was watching cartoons. After she hung up, Mrs. Evans came into the living room and turned off the TV. "Eli, your parents are on their way home," she said.

"What 'bout Ian?" I asked.

"I have some bad news, sweetheart," she said as she gently pulled me up onto her lap. "Ian won't be coming home with your mom and dad. The doctors and nurses did everything they could, but they couldn't fix him. Ian went to live with Jesus."

"Oh," I replied as the information sank in. "I hurt Ian! I'm a bad boy! Mommy and Daddy mad at me!" I yelled as I wriggled off of Mrs. Evans's lap and ran to my room.

She tried to console me, but it didn't work. That was the night the emptiness and anger in me started. I was angry at myself for causing Ian's death and angry at God for taking away my brother. Mom had said a prayer, but it didn't work. I knew things would never be the same.

I was drifting in and out of sleep when Mom and Dad got home. I could hear Mom crying while Dad explained to Mrs. Evans what happened. I heard him say, "It's my fault," and "I should have been watching the boys better." I heard Mrs. Evans try to console my parents by replying, "May God give you and your family comfort and strength during this difficult time." It didn't take the pain away.

I don't remember much about the next week. I guess I was still in a state of shock. There were so many people who came over to check on us—family members, friends, neighbors. I remember sitting in the front pew at the church with my parents. Ian's little white coffin was right in front of us surrounded by flowers and pictures of his smiling face. All I could think was, *Ian died because of me.* Even the comforting sermon the minister gave didn't help.

As the weeks went by, the tension in the house grew. Mom cried a lot, saying she should've been there when she was needed the most. Dad was so upset and distracted over everything it started to affect his job performance. Eventually, his boss told him to take some time off to cope with his loss.

The weeks turned into months, and Dad just couldn't pull himself together. I'm sure Mom never blamed him for what happened to Ian, but it didn't matter. Being in the house was too vivid of a reminder. We came home from a weekend trip to Aunt Bea's to find that Dad had packed up his things and left. He wrote a note saying he was sorry he failed as a father and as a husband, and he promised to come back when he could be what we needed and deserved. He promised to get another job and send money as soon as he got paid. I had just turned five, and that was the last time we heard from him.

Mom was devastated. As she tried to pick up the pieces of her life, she began to figure out just how bad things had gotten. She found stacks of bills in the desk, some with "past due" and "final notice" written on them. With no money coming in, Dad had used the savings and retirement accounts to pay the bills for as long as he could. Now they were empty, and bill collectors were starting to call.

At least they did until the phone company shut off our service. She tried to sell off what she could, but the bills just wouldn't stop. Even though we had insurance, the hospital and flight bills were staggering! Before she knew it, the house was being foreclosed on by the bank. She had to file for bankruptcy and start over. A single mother and broke, Mom figured that things could only get better. So when Aunt Bea told her about a small house for rent near her, we packed up the minivan and hit the road.

Junior must have figured I needed to take my own time to reflect on the past. He asked the rest of the group to quietly read a chapter in the Bible. It was the first time I had really let myself think about what happened. Even though the rest of the group didn't know the details, they didn't seem to judge me. From what I had already heard about their pasts, I fit right in. I didn't know what to think anymore.

The camp bell rang just as Junior was saying "Amen." The rest of the night was a blur. I had a difficult time staying focused at the bonfire. I could hear Trevor and the other campers singing, but all I could see was the scene from my childhood as it replayed in my head. I wondered what I should have done differently, not that I could have known any better. After all, I was only four. Doubt of my true responsibility started to creep into my mind. Maybe I really wasn't to blame. Maybe it was just a horrible accident.

Out of the corner of my eye, I saw Amber glance my way. She had a look of concern as if she knew what I was experiencing. I quickly looked away, too confused and too tired to think anymore. I was so grateful when we were dismissed. Without saying anything to the other campers, I returned to the cabin and crawled into my bunk in utter exhaustion. I closed my eyes and wished that morning wouldn't come.

CHAPTER 6

Yet again, the clanging of the bell and the commotion in the cabin woke me up at the crack of dawn. This time though, I got into the bathroom stalls and completed my cleaning assignment before anyone could use them. I wasn't about to make the same mistake I did yesterday.

During breakfast, I overheard my group talking about the plan for after school. Apparently, on Tuesday and Thursday afternoons, the campers had mandatory team-building exercises. Our Courage cabin members had to work with the Wisdom campers, and the girls from the Hope and Faith cabins would work together. I had already met some of the guys from the other cabin, and I knew they would irritate me. It turned out that today was the Ultimate Tug-of-War. It seemed like a fitting name for such a lame contest.

I didn't get too much grief from Ms. Reid during class. I figured if I flew under her radar and did the class work, then I wouldn't draw attention to myself. When she wasn't looking, I started to sketch a detailed map of the camp property. I hid the paper in my Bible after class and planned to work on it daily while I formulated an escape plan.

After class had ended for the day, all of the campers gathered on the central lawn where two long ropes were laid out—one for the boys and one for the girls. The center of each rope was marked with a red bandana, and there were chalk lines drawn on the grass fifteen feet from each side of the bandanas.

Junior started lining up our group along the south segment of the boys' rope. He stuck me at the front of the lineup opposite the guy I hated from class—Derek. Like me, he was fairly new to the camp and still adjusting to the way things operated around here. He was from a rough upbringing and had a huge chip on his shoulder. From the challenging look he gave me, I knew this was gonna be a fight to the finish. *The guys behind me on the rope better be prepared.* I dug my heels into the grass.

Glancing to my right, I realized Amber was also positioned at the front of her cabin's rope. I gave her an encouraging nod to which she responded back. Her hair was braided down her back with a few wisps gently blowing around her face. I hadn't noticed before that she wore thick bracelets around her wrists. I was so distracted with curiosity I almost didn't hear Trevor announcing the start of the contest.

"Ready! Set! Go!" Trevor yelled as he wildly swung the starting flag in the air.

Every muscle in my body tightened as I pulled on the rope. I knew I wouldn't get much help out of my team members. Most of them were weak. Seeing Derek opposite me with a smug grin on his face made me want to win even more. My arms and legs ached as I fought to maintain our field position.

"Come on, guys! Pull together as a team!" Junior yelled from the sidelines.

My muscles burned, my heart pounded, and the sweat dripping down my forehead threatened to sting my eyes. No matter how hard I pulled, we were gradually dragged toward the field's midline. I could hear my teammates grunting as they tried to help, slowly losing ground and energy with each heaving breath.

Before I knew what happened, Carter tripped into Zack and started a snowball effect. We all pitched forward and were dragged on our bellies across the line by the other team. Luckily, the grass kept the skin abrasions down to a minimum. The loss still hurt; my pride was thrashed. I could hear Derek cheering in celebration of his team's win. In my mind, I took it as a personal attack.

With my last bit of energy, I leapt off the ground and ran at Derek. He had no time to react or prepare for my retaliation. Our eyes were locked in a stare-down as my right fist connected with his jawbone. The force from my hit knocked him off his feet. I heard the crowd gasp as Vaughn lunged forward and grabbed me before I hit Derek again.

The shocked look on Amber's face told me I probably shouldn't have done that. But I didn't care. I wasn't gonna let Derek make a fool out of me!

Junior and the guard I met earlier rushed over and relieved Vaughn. They held me until I quit struggling. Meanwhile, Trevor told Derek's counselor to take him to the nurse's office while he dismissed the rest of the campers to their cabins to wait until dinner.

I was taken to the Solitary Reflection Room attached to the security guards' cabin. It was a small room with a bed, light, sink, and toilet. The wall that connected my room and the guards' cabin was made of metal bars and had a sliding door. A little bit of outdoor light filtered in through a long, narrow window at the top of my cell. Trevor and Junior led me into the cell and shut the door with a thud. I suddenly felt like I was in prison. There was no privacy, no escape.

Junior stood quietly in the corner of the guards' cabin, knowing that Trevor would know what to say to me. The security guard told Junior he would be back in a bit.

"I'm sorry I have to put you here for the night," Trevor said. "This room is utilized only in extreme circumstances. There are no outside distractions, and it gives you time to unwind and reflect upon where you've been and where you're going. It breaks my heart when campers make poor choices and wind up here, especially you, Eli. The counselors and I are usually able to help the campers through their problems and get their lives back on track. I must be reminded sometimes though, that it's the Almighty who heals the broken."

I couldn't look at Trevor as he reprimanded and lectured me. I was so angry! I hated everybody!

"Can I have my Bible?" I bellowed at him, hoping to spend the evening working on my map of the camp.

"I'm sorry," Trevor responded. "I can't let you return to the cabin to retrieve yours, but I will lend you mine. This is the Bible I received when I was in prison," he said as he passed it to me between the bars. "You can still see the notes I wrote in the margins."

"What'd you do to wind up behind bars?" I asked.

"Back in the day, I did some stupid things. I thought I could change. I married a nice woman and had a son and daughter, but I still made bad choices. That's what I grew up with and all I knew. I wanted to give my family a better financial future, so I robbed a bank at gunpoint and was sent to prison. I took the easy way out, and it cost me everything. My wife left me and took my kids away. I never saw any of them again. In a weird way, it was the best thing that could have happened to me. I met Junior in prison, became a Christian, and got a whole new outlook on life. I hoped I could be reunited with my family, but it was too late. Not long after I finished my sentence, the last of my family passed away. I never got to say I was sorry."

The security guard returned to the cabin with two plates of dinner. "The other guy will be fine," he said. "The nurse and counselor took him to the clinic in town. No broken bones, just bruising." He set his plate down on a table and unlocked the door to my cell. He opened the door wide enough to pass the plate in, but I refused to take it.

"It's here if you want it," he said as he put my dinner plate on the floor and slid the door shut. The click of the lock made my stomach turn.

"Well, I'd better head to the main lodge to deliver the dinner prayer. Please utilize this time to think about how your actions affected others and what different choices you could've made. I'll see you in the morning." Before I could say anything, he turned around and left with Junior not far behind.

"If I were you," said the guard, "I would eat and get started on some soul searchin'. It's gonna be a long night."

"Whatever!" I retorted.

I left the plate on the floor and flopped down onto the uncomfortable bed. The food smelled delicious, but I wasn't about to give him the satisfaction of being right.

"All right then," he said, "since we're gonna be cabin mates for the night, I might as well introduce myself. I'm Gabe. I'm sure you probably hate me for changing your look when you first got here. That's okay. Eventually, you'll understand that people only camouflage their internal torments when they try to deface what God gave them. Here, we put everyone on a level playing field, help them to conquer their demons and move on with their lives."

"I have nothin' to say to you," I responded flatly and rolled over onto my side so I didn't have to look at him through the bars.

"I hope you don't mind, but I sing to myself when I don't have anyone to talk with," Gabe replied.

I didn't answer. I hoped he would just leave me alone. At least being locked up overnight meant I didn't have to attend our cabin meeting. I did, however, regret I wouldn't be able to see Amber at the bonfire.

And then the most unexpected thing happened. Gabe reclined back on one of the three guards' bunks and started to sing the most beautiful gospel song I had ever heard. He sounded like an absolute angel.

I tried to ignore Gabe, so I opened the Bible Trevor let me borrow. As I flipped through the chapters, I could see his notes in pencil in the margins—forgiveness, grace, peace, eternity. The words he wrote almost captured my interest for wanting to read about why he wrote these particular words in the margins—almost.

Instead, I chose to shut the book and close my eyes. I decided to sleep through my discipline rather than face it. I could still hear Gabe quietly singing as the late-afternoon light flickered through the window above my bed. I figured the bonfire sing-along would be starting soon. *I don't care. At least I'll get caught up on some sleep.* The 6:00 p.m. to 6:00 a.m. guard would be returning to the cabin shortly after dawn, and the third guard had the noon-midnight shift. Since Gabe worked the 6:00 a.m. to 6:00 p.m. shift, I guess that meant he was pulling a double shift that night to make sure I stayed out of trouble. My anticipation of a restful night didn't last long.

I tossed and turned for what seemed like hours before I finally sank into a fitful sleep. My dream transported me back to the day of Ian's drowning, reliving the trauma from a third-person perspective. I watched as his gleeful grin turned into an expression of sheer panic and terror as he fought to keep his head above the water. I could see him flail and gasp and heard him cry out, "Eli, help! Cold!"

I could feel my heart race, and a lump form in my throat as I watched myself run to get help. The feeling of helplessness and guilt were overwhelming as my four-year-old self observed the resuscitation attempts. I was angry at myself for not being a better brother, angry at my parents, the paramedics, the doctors, and the nurses for not being able to save Ian! Mostly though, I was angry at God! He took away my only sibling! Ian was my best friend and didn't deserve this to happen to him!

It was then I noticed something unusual. I don't remember seeing it on the day of the accident. Maybe I was too young to perceive it, or maybe I had blocked it from my memory. As Mom knelt down in the snow next to Ian, an angel appeared beside my brother. He had an amazing light around him. He stayed with Ian even during the flight to the hospital. Ian had a peaceful look on his face when I saw him for the last time. There was no look of pain or fear.

Then, I could see myself as I sat in the front row at the funeral. Invisible to me at the time was an adorable young boy who stood beside the coffin in a white suit. He had a glow just like the angel that appeared by Ian at the pond.

And then he spoke, "I forgive you, Eli. It wasn't your fault. I'm okay. Don't worry about me."

All wrapped up in the sheet from my fitful sleep, I fell off the bed with a thud. I was drenched in sweat, my heart pounded through my chest wall, and my mind reeled. *That felt too real to be a dream.* I looked over at Gabe where he was still reclined on his bunk, singing to himself. The clock on the wall indicated it was only ten minutes later than when I first shut the Bible and closed my eyes.

Gabe looked over at me with a reassuring smile and said, "He has risen." He then turned over and went to sleep.

I was reluctant to go to sleep, afraid of what else I might dream. So I turned on my light and started reading the chapters of the Bible where Trevor had written in the margins. I read portions of Genesis, Psalms, Proverbs, and the first four books of the New Testament. I was getting sleepy, but the more I read, the more I wanted to read. I finally drifted off to sleep in the early hours of the morning. There were no further dreams or nightmares, just peaceful sleep.

CHAPTER 7

I thought I would get out of chores while I was in solitary confinement. I was wrong. Gabe was up and around while it was still dark outside. The guard whose shift ended at midnight snored softly in his bunk. I tried to ignore Gabe when he told me to wake up, but he didn't take that very well. He opened the sliding door and pulled the sheet off me.

"I said get up!" he demanded in a loud, stern voice.

"Fine!" I shouted back at him as I sat up and rubbed my eyes.

"I hope you have a better day today. Did you learn anything about yourself during your overnight stay here?"

I pretended I didn't hear him. I wasn't going to tell him about my dream or the fact that I had actually read some of the Bible.

My disrespectful behavior didn't affect Gabe at all. "Selective hearing doesn't work with me, Mr. Parker. I'm taking you to your cabin on my way to work. You should get back just in time to do your chores and get ready for the day. By the way, Eli, a little bird told me that Ian never blamed you for what happened. You should stop blaming yourself."

How did he know about any of that? Unless Junior or the other campers broke the agreement of confidentiality, there's no way he could know about what happened.

I followed Gabe across the property to the Courage cabin and went in. Everyone was just waking up.

"Nice to have you back, Eli," Junior said.

Several of the guys said "good morning" and "glad you're back" as I settled into the usual routine. I didn't want to talk about what happened though, so I grabbed the cleaning supplies and headed to the stalls. I finished early enough and was the first one in line for the shower. At least I didn't wind up with cold water like the previous morning.

The rest of the morning was uneventful. I spent every spare minute in class working on the map when Ms. Reid wasn't looking. I was determined to find a way out of here one way or another.

During the lunch hour, I figured I would ask Kalvin for some information. I pulled him to the side where nobody else would hear our conversation.

"Hey, man," I said to him. "Has anyone ever gotten out of here before their scheduled sentence was up?"

"Nah," he replied. "I've thought about it, but the idea of spendin' the night in the woods kinda freaked me out. I'm not exactly the campin' type."

"If someone didn't mind the outdoors," I persisted, "what would be the best option? Hypothetically speaking," I added.

"Of course, man. On the down low, the security cameras are placed everywhere. The guards roam the campus at all hours, and the fence extends around the entire camp. The only way in or out is through the main gate."

"Is there ever a time it's left open?" I asked.

"Every Friday, a truck brings supplies from town. Good luck to you." He nodded to me, and I knew our conversation was over. Short and to the point. We didn't want to draw too much attention to either of us.

I headed back to class and finished out the school day, hopeful there might be an opportunity for an unexpected early release. I didn't even complain to Eddie about going to the tutoring session. What seemed odd to me was the more I learned, the more I wanted to learn. I guess being surrounded by people focused on self-improvement and doing the right thing was starting to rub off on me. All of my friends back home were only interested in self-destructive behaviors and causing trouble.

I made it through dinner without any major issues. Derek glanced my way and gave me a nod. I couldn't tell if he was trying to start another fight or if he was just indicating he was over what I did to him; the swelling and bruising were pretty bad. It didn't matter to me either way. Forgiveness was a foreign concept to me.

My attention was diverted to Amber. I could see her sitting at a table across the room. Her cabin members were trying to get her to join their conversations, but she kept her eyes fixed on her dinner plate as she ate. She acted like she couldn't hear anyone. The rumor was that she still hadn't said a word since she had arrived at New Beginnings Camp. It was like she was in a protective bubble where nobody could hurt her.

She looked up and met my gaze when she realized I had been staring at her. A pink flush crept into her cheeks, but she didn't look away. The blank stare briefly faded, and a shy smile appeared on her lips. Amber's icy shield began to melt. Maybe we were brought together by fate to help each other heal.

As her group got up from their table and prepared to head to their evening chat, Amber gave me a quick wave. I almost skipped to my cabin to get my Bible for my own group meeting. This summer might not be looking so bad after all!

I joined everyone under our usual tree not dreading the group session as much as the previous evenings. I even listened to what some of the other guys were saying as I looked forward to being at the amphitheater tonight. Matt helped a new camper get settled into the Wisdom cabin. Carter learned how to shoe a horse. Zack had his weekly weigh in with the nurse, and he had dropped ten pounds since his arrival at camp. Kalvin had earned some extra money helping with yard work and maintenance around the camp, and he was putting that toward what he owed to the people he swindled back home. Mason reached his six month anniversary for being clean and sober. Bo received word that his baby would arrive soon, and he would be allowed to go to the hospital to be with his girlfriend when the time came. Vaughn was able to walk away from a disagreement with another camper rather than engage in a fight. Eddie had several of the campers he tutored pass the GED. And finally came Max. He received a letter from his family saying how they were heartbroken over him running away and begged him to return home to meet his new sister.

"How about you, Eli," Junior addressed me as my turn came up. "What would you like to talk about tonight?"

I thought for a moment and then I responded, "No offense to anybody, but I can't wait to get back home."

"I'm sure you're not the only one," replied Junior. "Trevor and Judge Mosaron will decide when you will be released. How long that takes is up to you."

The bell rang just as Junior finished his prayer. We returned to the cabin to put our Bibles away then headed to the amphitheater for singing around the bonfire. The songs were getting stuck in my head, and I found myself paying attention to the lyrics and their meanings. They were about unconditional love, forgiveness, grace, and trust. I vaguely remembered about how these related to a guy named Jesus from the Sunday-school classes I went to as a kid. I couldn't remember the specifics. I had spent too many years trying to forget.

When I reached the amphitheater, I realized there was an open seat next to Amber. She patted the seat as she saw me walking her way indicating she had saved it specifically for me. She actually liked me! I was so excited I didn't watch where I was walking. I tripped over a tree root and landed right at her feet. My clumsiness could ruin everything. *I'm an idiot! I just blew my chance with Amber!*

To my surprise, she reached down and helped me off the ground. My face was beet red and throbbing from embarrassment as she brushed the dirt from my clothing and checked for injuries. She seemed to want to say something as our eyes met, but she remained silent.

"Thank you," I muttered as I tried to regain my composure.

She replied with a thumbs up gesture and a "you're welcome" smile.

We remained standing as the music played and the other campers sang. Dusk had settled into the camp, and the twinkling of the stars danced against the pink-and-purple hues of the sky. The bonfire was radiating heat, but nothing compared to the warmth I felt as Amber gently placed her hand in mine. My heart raced. It felt like everything was perfect.

I could feel her bracelet against my wrist, and in the dim light, I could see some designs on it. She wore similar bracelets on each wrist. Amber's muscles tensed as she realized what I was looking at. She tried to pull away, but I kept a firm, reassuring grip on her hand.

"It's okay if you have problems in your past," I whispered into her ear. "I've had my own issues to deal with. I've lost close family members and made some pretty stupid decisions growing up. You don't have to tell me if you don't want to, but I'll be here if you ever need to talk."

As she listened to what I said, her tense muscles began to relax. It was as if she finally found someone who truly understood the depth of her pain and despair. We spent the remainder of the evening listening to the music with our hands clasped together. Even though neither of us knew about what each other had been through, there was an unspoken understanding and bond.

At the close of the evening, I walked Amber back to her cabin. I told her everything would be all right and to not worry about whatever was bothering her. I don't know why I felt like saying that when I was still trying to conquer my own past. It just seemed like the right thing to say for both of us.

CHAPTER 8

I made it through my chores and was the first in my cabin to shower and get dressed. I got to the dining hall, had my plate loaded with food, and sat at my assigned table before most of the other campers had finished getting themselves ready for the day. I got there early enough to watch Amber, to see if last night was just another episode of my overactive imagination.

She grinned and waved at me as she got her breakfast and made her way over to her table with her cabin mates. *Hallelujah! I wasn't dreaming!*

For the first time since arriving, I bowed my head and closed my eyes during Trevor's blessing of the food. It didn't feel weird to do. I even said "Amen" at the end of the prayer, just like everyone else. Everyone, that is, except Amber.

Trevor's morning announcement informed us of that afternoon's team-building activity—the ropes course. I forgot to mention to Junior that I was deathly afraid of heights! There was no way I would be able to make it through that activity! I would just have to find a way out of it.

We were dismissed to our cabins to gather our supplies for class. I tried to explain my fear to Trevor, but he said it was mandatory for everyone to complete the exercise before their sentences were finished.

I thought back to the time when I was around seven years old. It was a hot summer day, similar to today, when I fell out of Aunt Bea's apple tree. I was trying to get to the upper branches where I had seen a bird's nest from the upstairs window. I was determined to see if there were any eggs inside the nest.

I had carefully climbed up the tree, picking my route from one branch to the next. The ripening apples smelled so sweet, and the shade from the leaves kept me cool as I went higher and higher. There was no fear in me, even though I had never climbed that high before.

Just as I neared the object of my interest, I heard the branch beneath me crack. I reached up to grab hold of a limb to steady myself, but I ended up grabbing the bird's nest instead. Before I knew what happened, the branch I was standing on broke. I pulled the nest close to my chest as I fell backward. I could see the sun filtering down through the apple leaves as I hurtled toward the ground. I think I hit every branch on the way down. Time seemed to have slowed, and my senses became more acute as I fell. I wondered if I was gonna die like Ian. *Would it hurt? Would I see a bright light? Was there a heaven?* I had watched some of those talk shows with Aunt Bea, and some of the guests on the TV swore they had near-death experiences. They were certain there was more than just the here and now.

And then it happened. I hit the ground with such a thud it knocked the wind out of me and caused me to briefly black out. My head and whole body ached. When I opened my eyes, everything was blurry. I saw a boy standing over me, and I heard him say, "You'll be okay, Eli."

I closed my eyes again. *Was I alive or was I dead?* I was sure I had seen Ian standing by me, but that was impossible. Ian had been gone for over three years.

I could vaguely hear another voice yelling, "Eli! Are you okay?" I opened my eyes again to see Aunt Bea running across the yard to me. She had thrown the jar of sun tea she was taking into the house when she heard the branch snap and saw me fall.

She dropped to the ground next to me, breathless and sweating profusely. "Let me check you over," she said as she assessed me from head to toe. When she was finished, she said, "I don't think any bones are broken, but I'm taking you in to check your noggin. Make sure you don't have a concussion."

"What's this?" Aunt Bea asked as she removed the nest from my grip.

"Oh!" I moaned as I slowly sat up. "I was looking for bird eggs. Are there any in there?"

We peered into the nest and could see several cracked shells. Then we saw something unexpected. In the corner of the nest protected by grass and leaves was a tiny bird.

"Well, would you look at that?" Aunt Bea exclaimed. "It looks like a baby finch!" As she carefully picked it up, she could tell there was something wrong. "It looks like it has a hurt wing!"

"Will it be okay?" I anxiously asked, completely forgetting about my own aches and pains.

"Let's see what we can do to help it. Do you think you can walk to the house?" she asked as she gently helped me up from the ground.

"I think so," I bravely responded. I fought back tears, not so much from the pain caused by my sprained ankle as the thought I had hurt another innocent baby. I carefully cradled it next to my chest the whole way back.

When we got into the house, Aunt Bea had me rest on the couch while she wrapped my ankle and put ice on it. I was so glad she was there to help me. Mom was still at work and wouldn't be home for hours. I told Aunt Bea to not worry Mom by calling her at work to explain what happened. She was still trying to cope with Ian's death, Dad leaving, and having to start her life over.

"I think his wing will mend if we can splint it. Then, it will be up to us to be his temporary mama. Do you think you can help feed and care for it?"

"Yup!" I happily answered. "Let's name him Birdy."

"Sounds good!" Aunt Bea chuckled as she gently splinted the wing with a Popsicle stick and some medical tape. "There! If that doesn't work, then I don't know what will," she said as she finished putting Birdy back together.

"I'll go find some worms and a box for him, then we'll head into town to check out your head."

While Aunt Bea was outside, I looked Birdy in the eyes and told him how sorry I was for hurting him. I told him I would do whatever was needed for him to get better.

When she returned, Aunt Bea mashed up some worms and put them into a small dropper. I fed Birdy and was amazed at how he tilted his head upward to take the food I offered. When I placed him into the cardboard box, he seemed to be getting around okay with his wing splinted.

It took us about two hours to get to town and back. The doctor said I had a mild concussion but no fractures in my ankle. He said that somebody upstairs was looking out for me that day, and I was lucky to be alive.

It took several weeks of round-the-clock feedings for Birdy to heal. Each day, he got a little stronger, and his downy covering became beautiful yellow feathers. His little chirps gradually turned into pleasant music. Soon, he began to flap his wings, exercising them in anticipation of returning to his family.

When the time finally came, Aunt Bea gently cut the splint from Birdy's wing. I sadly watched as he flapped his wings and, after a few awkward attempts, fly away. "Bye," I whispered as I tried to be brave. I knew he would be better off with his own kind, but I still put food out for the remainder of the summer, hoping he would return. Aunt Bea said she would sometimes hear him singing in the trees while she was doing dishes with the kitchen window open. I think he was singing thank you to both of us for fixing him.

I had been so distracted by the news of today's upcoming challenge that I was late for class. Papers flew from my binder as I ran across the yard. This delayed me even more as I stopped to retrieve them. Apparently, the binder rings didn't lock together when I hid the map. Just my luck!

I rushed into the classroom breathless and flopped down in my chair just after the bell rang. My binder tumbled off the desk and papers scattered across the floor. Flustered by my not-so-graceful entrance, I scrambled to pick them up. Amber's seat was right behind mine, and I thanked her as she handed me a stack she retrieved from under her desk.

Ms. Reid gave me a disapproving glare at my disheveled appearance and disruptive behavior. "I'm glad you could join us, Mr. Parker," she addressed me. "I was just explaining to the class that we will be learning some physics before our regular lessons to expand on today's team-building activity. Class, please take out some paper, and open your science textbooks to page 182."

As I looked through my binder for some blank paper, I began to silently panic. *Where's my map? I know I put it in here at the cabin! Did I drop it on the yard? Did someone find it? Would anyone know I drew it as an escape plan? I'm so dead!*

"Is there a problem, Mr. Parker?" Ms. Reid asked with impatience in her voice.

"No, sir, I mean ma'am," I stammered as I tried to compose myself. I could hear snickers from the rest of the class at my response.

"Good," she replied then began teaching about gravity, momentum, and inertia.

I tried to focus on what was being taught, but my mind was racing. That map was my golden ticket out of here! I didn't have a photographic memory, and I sure didn't have any outdoor experience or survival skills. Now what? The best I could hope for was none of the staff had found the map. It would definitely mean game over for me. I would wind up doing real time for sure!

During class and the lunch break, I thought about where my map could be. I listened into lunchtime conversations with the hope that somebody might mention it. No such luck. I would either have to make do with what details I could remember, or I would have to come up with another plan. My careless mistake was an epic disaster!

CHAPTER 9

I should have been glad class was done for the day, but I wasn't. My absolute dread and fear of heights had me so uptight I felt sick to my stomach. I didn't even know what the ropes course would involve, but I was almost desperate enough to pick a fight with someone to get sent back to solitary.

"Hey, everyone," Junior addressed the Courage cabin members when we returned to put our school supplies away and prepare for the challenge. "I want you all to gather around."

As we formed a circle in the cabin, Junior bowed his head and said, "Let us pray." Everybody, including me, followed his lead. "Father, we ask that you watch over each of us today as we face our fears to overcome the obstacles in our paths. Strengthen our bodies and our minds to know you are right there with us, helping us during the difficult times and carrying us when we feel unable to continue. Keep us safe and ever mindful of your presence. This we ask in Jesus' name, Amen."

Junior looked around at each of the campers. "I have faith that every one of you will complete the course today. Size doesn't matter. Will and determination do. Are you ready to go out there and do this to prove to yourselves you're all winners?" Junior asked as he put his arm into the circle to get the team spirit pumped up.

I looked around at my teammates, and they looked at me. One by one, we put our arms in to join Junior. With each arm added, I could feel the camaraderie strengthen.

"Okay, guys," Junior said. "Go, team Courage, on the count of three. One. Two. Three." Following that intro, the loudest, unified roar I had ever heard erupted from our group. Everyone became filled with excitement and anticipation. Our gang of misfits actually sounded like a team.

We flung the cabin door open and ran to the course at the edge of the campus. I could see the groups from the other three cabins already gathered with their counselors. Trevor stood in front of the groups, waiting for everyone to arrive before he explained the rules of the challenge.

"Welcome to the challenge," Trevor addressed the crowd. "Today, you will be testing your strength, endurance, and problem-solving skills. It will take teamwork and good communication to complete the challenge. I have paired the boys' cabins with the girls' cabins. Courage cabin will work with Faith and Wisdom cabin with Hope. I expect everyone to wear the safety harnesses and helmets we'll be passing out. Your counselors will be positioned around the course to ensure your safety and provide encouragement. I trust in your abilities. Believe in yourselves and have faith in the Lord."

For some reason, that speech didn't make me any less afraid of heights!

As we were putting on our helmets and safety harnesses, Trevor explained the course. We were to start by walking across a rope suspended two feet off the ground. Next, we would attach our harnesses to a security line and climb a cargo net that appeared to be thirty feet high. Then, we needed to transfer our harnesses to a zip line and slide down to the bottom. There were two suspended ropes for each of the groups to cross, but the cargo net and zip line had to be utilized by both groups. This was definitely going to be a feat in sharing. Trevor said the activity wasn't timed, but we would all need to complete the course before dinner. It didn't matter how we determined what order we would compete in, we just needed to come up with a game plan.

"You all have five minutes to talk with your teammates to work out a strategy," Trevor advised us.

Quickly, the assigned groups gathered together and started brainstorming.

"I think we should go youngest to oldest," volunteered a blonde-haired girl.

"That's lame," said Vaughn. "What if they can't make it to the top or freak out? Then we'd never finish."

"What about girls first?" asked Carter.

"Why?" questioned a girl with short brunette hair. "Are you chicken?"

I listened to the back-and-forth ideas and criticisms, knowing that our time was running out. "What about alternating?" I suggested. "If we space out the younger and weaker members with those who are older and stronger, we would have a better chance for everyone to get through the course." Where did that idea come from? I was never good at working with a group unless it was to cause trouble. I was more of a loner, an outcast.

Amber looked surprised and impressed the suggestion came out of my mouth.

"What a great idea!" Eddie commented. "If we send a strong member up first, they could show the group how to perform the maneuver and help those who need it."

We finished our brainstorming just in time. Trevor blew a whistle and gathered the two large groups together to the starting line. We quickly arranged our group of twenty into a fairly even lineup. Bo was up first, followed by some of the girls and younger kids. I was elected to go last, right behind Amber. My anxiety worsened as I realized everyone would rely on me to finish the course. *What if I fail? I would let my whole team down.*

"Ready. Set. Go!" shouted Trevor to start the challenge.

Bo took off across the suspended rope without any problems. He used his arms to maintain his balance and reached the end before the other team. Unlike the other team though, he stopped to encourage the kids behind him. When the girl behind him fell off the rope, he cheered her on while the counselor helped her back up. He then waited for Zack to clumsily make his way to the end.

When these three had finished the first portion of the course, they ran over to the cargo net, and the next group began the challenge. Each member of our team shouted words of encouragement as Bo started to climb the intertwined ropes. He scaled approximately one-third of the distance then waited for the girl and Zack to secure their harnesses and climb up to meet him. By the time they reached the top section of the cargo net, the girl and Zack were getting tired. Bo reached down and was able to help each of them climb the last few feet to the top.

As they rested on the platform, Bo and his group turned to look down at the competitors just starting across the suspended rope and those on the cargo net. "You can do it!" they cheered.

The counselor on the platform helped transfer the safety harnesses from the security line to the zip line. The other team already had one person slide to the bottom. They were ahead of us, but their strategy was different from ours. They seemed to be performing as individuals rather than as a team.

Bo was the first of our group to complete the course. Junior waited at the bottom to help everyone safely descend the line.

"Great job!" Junior praised the campers as they reached the ground and removed their helmets and harnesses.

"We did it!" Bo rejoiced, giving high fives to his teammates as they finished.

From the last position in line, I watched and waited. I saw the techniques that Bo initiated work for the groups that followed. But the longer I waited, the more nervous I became. I was afraid I wouldn't be able to hide my fear. *What would Amber think of me if I choke or can't finish?* I knew the other team was way ahead of us, so the pressure of being last was giving me a knot in my stomach.

Six groups of three and then it was just Amber and me. She practically flew across the suspended rope, almost like her feet barely touched it. Her balance was amazing! After jumping to the ground, she turned to wait for me.

I was never good at sports or anything athletic for that matter. The rope bounced and swayed as I desperately swung my arms around to maintain my balance. Even that distance off the ground made me woozy. I glanced up to see Amber waving, trying to get my attention. She tilted her chin upward, held her back straight, kept her arms out to the side, and looked ahead. Slow and steady, she put one foot in front of the other, mimicking how to cross the suspended rope.

Amber's calm demeanor helped me refocus on the task at hand. I copied her movements and was across the rope before I knew it. I was thrilled! The worst was yet to come, though.

As we sprinted over to the cargo net, I could hear our teammates cheering. I felt almost uplifted and confident, then reality put me in check.

I watched Amber attach her harness to the security line and gracefully ascend the cargo net. As with the previous groups, she turned to me and waited for me to do the same. Unfortunately, she made it look easier than it was. I attached my harness to the line and began to haul myself up the net. My legs and arms felt like rubber by the time we reached the second stopping point.

It was then, in the midst of my exhaustion, I did something that nearly cost me my life: I looked down. In the instant I did that, I panicked. Everything began to spin. I felt like I couldn't breathe. My hands became so sweaty that my grip started to slip. One finger at a time came loose until I was down to my index fingers. My ability to hold on was gone. I closed my eyes.

Just as my grip failed, I felt a tight grasp on each wrist. When I opened my eyes, holding onto each wrist were Amber and Derek. Like me, Derek was the last in line to start the course. He was climbing the cargo net at the same time as we were and was at the right place at the right time.

"You okay?" Derek asked as he helped me regain my grip and footing on the net.

"I think so," I answered, realizing how close I had been to falling. "Thank you both." I gratefully acknowledged their heroic act, not knowing until we all reached the top of the net that in my nervous haste at the bottom, I hadn't properly secured my harness to the security line.

"I owe you both. I would've fallen and probably died if you weren't there to catch me."

"That's what friends do. They watch your back," said Derek with a sarcastic tone. He then attached his harness to the zip line and sped to the bottom.

"Are you ready?" I asked Amber as she prepared for the last part of the course.

She looked as if she was about to say something, but then she changed her mind. Down the line she went, leaving me as the last remaining person to complete the challenge.

You can do this. Face your fear. I heard the dinner bell ringing in the background, and I knew it was now or never.

How else was I supposed to get down? The cargo net? Not a chance!

I attached my harness to the line and stepped to the edge of the platform. I started to look down, but I decided I didn't want to get dizzy again. Instead, I closed my eyes and said a quick and spontaneous, "God, please keep me safe." I heard the crowd below clapping and cheering words of encouragement.

And then I did it. With my eyes still closed and my hands clutching my harness, I stepped off the platform into a space of nothingness. I could feel the air rushing against my face and hear the zing of the safety clip against the line. I smelled the trees and felt the temperature changes on my skin as I entered and exited shaded areas. It was like time had slowed down, even though I knew I was hurtling down the line at a fast rate.

I opened my eyes just as I reached the bottom. Junior gave me a celebratory pat on the back, and everyone else, including the members of the other team, gave me high fives. When I looked back at the platform, it surprised me just how high up it was. *I did it! I faced my fears!*

"Nice job, Eli! I'm so proud of your achievement!" Trevor said as he approached me with his hand outstretched.

"Thanks!" I responded, accepting and returning the handshake.

The dinner bell rang again, indicating we had better get moving. We sprinted to the main building, dished up, and sat down in record time. After such a physically demanding afternoon, we were all ravenous.

"I would like to tell everyone how impressed I was with their performance at today's challenge," Trevor addressed us as we tried to patiently wait for him to bless the food. "Each rope is made up of many strands that by themselves wouldn't be able to withstand much tension. Intertwined together though, so much more can be accomplished. It's just like people. When we work together and have God on our side, anything is possible."

We nearly inhaled our meals as soon as the blessing was said. Once our bellies were full, the boisterous chatter from every table was very noisy. Everyone was relaying their scariest moments and the events of the day that had been their biggest triumphs. Even I was involved in the conversations. My play-by-play of nearly falling to my death had my entire table riveted! This was definitely one of those stories that would be retold for years to come!

After dinner, we grabbed our Bibles and headed to our usual spot under the tree. Everyone spoke about their performance at the challenge today. For most of my group, this was the biggest challenge they had faced and successfully overcome.

"What about you, Eli?" Junior asked. "What would you like to share tonight?"

I thought for a long moment before I spoke. I looked Junior in the eyes, and I responded, "I prayed for the first time since I was a kid. This time, God answered my prayer."

"That's awesome!" Junior said. "I'm glad to see your faith is being restored."

We finished our discussion time and prepared to go to the amphitheater. I couldn't wait to talk with Amber to tell her "thank you" again. I didn't expect that I wouldn't get the chance.

When I got down to the amphitheater, I noticed there were no empty seats anywhere near Amber. I saw her look my way when I approached the benches, but then she quickly looked away. She acted like she didn't even know me! I was hurt and confused. Just when I thought she was into me, she changed the game!

I decided I wasn't about to waste any more time getting too close to people. All they ever did was let me down. From now on, I was relying on nobody but me. It was time to return to my mission of getting out of here.

CHAPTER 10

I woke up early and quietly completed my assigned chore before anyone else. It was encouraging to know I was nearly done with being the newbie and the toilet duty that came with the title. However, the inner anger was back, and my fire to escape reignited within me.

My map had my escape route and the landmark representations on it. With it missing, I would have to figure out another way to shorten my stay at New Beginnings Camp. I had tried to scout the area while I was up on the cargo net and platform the day before, but I was too distracted by my fear of heights to really pay attention to the areas on the other side of the wall.

I remembered what Kalvin had told me earlier in the week. It was Friday, so the delivery truck would be by sometime today. Maybe I could hide inside or hang onto the frame underneath the truck to get outside the gate. I had seen lots of action movies with daring escapes, and I was convinced I could do just like the movie characters. I guess I hadn't thought about the details or the fact that the stunts were choreographed and performed by professionals.

Whatever, it was apparent nobody cared about me. No matter the risk to my health and safety, I wasn't about to stick around any longer.

I finished getting ready just as the wake-up bell started ringing. That particular day though, it sounded different. Rather than being rung five times, it continued for several minutes. I peeked out the window and could see staff run from one cabin to the next. I opened the door just as Trevor ran up the steps of the Courage cabin.

"Has anyone seen Amber from Hope cabin? Her counselor said she was gone when they woke up this morning. She didn't have anything except the clothes she was wearing."

Trevor sounded frantic. It was dangerous for an inexperienced person to be alone in this climate and environment, especially a girl.

"I saw her at the campfire last night, but I didn't talk to her. She gave me the cold shoulder," I answered.

"I need everyone's help right now," Trevor said. "The National Weather Service has put out an alert that there is a fast-moving storm headed our way. I don't know how long Amber has been gone, but she couldn't have gotten very far. I have the girls checking all cabins and buildings. The boys from Wisdom cabin are checking the barn, stalls, and all outdoor activity areas. The guards are reviewing the surveillance tapes and have contacted law enforcement for extra help. I need your group to check the perimeter to make sure she didn't find some area in the fence to escape.

"I trust that none of you will use this situation to make your own attempt at leaving. The surrounding terrain is extremely dangerous with steep drop-offs and the fierce McKenzie River. Hurry and go find Amber before the storm gets here."

We ran to check the fence line—half in one direction and half in the other—with the intent of meeting in the middle. It dawned on me that my missing map may be with Amber. I remembered I had made notes in the margins, and there was only one place she could have gone.

I took off running toward the place Eddie and I went for our tutoring sessions. As I looked up through the tree branches, I could see dark, ominous clouds. Until now, the weather during the week had been beautiful and warm. The roll of thunder in the distance provided the stark reality of how quickly the weather can change in the mountains.

As I approached the creek, I called out Amber's name. Not that I expected her to answer me, considering she still hadn't said a word to anyone since she got here. I followed the creek to where it met the wall. There was a culvert that had been built into the perimeter wall, which allowed the creek to flow to the point where it converged with the McKenzie. The water level was just a shallow trickle, but I knew the upcoming rain would soon make it an impassable route.

As I ducked down and made my way through the culvert, something in the water caught my attention. I reached down and retrieved it. To my surprise, it was one of Amber's bracelets! It was a thick metal band with intricate floral designs engraved on the exterior surface. The metal hinge was broken, which made it easier to read what was written on the inside: "Jade, my sister and best friend. Gone but not forgotten."

"Poor Amber," I said to myself. I knew what it was like to lose a sibling. I had to find her and tell her I knew what she was going through.

Even though it was early morning and should have been light and bright, the forest was becoming very dark and eerie as the storm approached. Without warning, a streak of lightning hit a tree not far from where I stood. I felt the hair stand up on the back of my neck as I dropped to the ground to avoid the flying tree bark. The deafening boom of the thunder that followed shook every part of my body.

"Amber!" I screamed as I resumed my frantic search. "Can you hear me?"

I scrambled over fallen trees and through the thick underbrush. The rain came down in torrents, and the wind howled through the trees.

I started to panic. *What if I couldn't find Amber? What if we die out here?* My mind was racing.

"Amber!" I yelled over and over. My pace was now a near sprint. The lightning and thunder were directly overhead. The rain pelted my face, and I couldn't see more than a few feet ahead of me.

In the distance, I could hear a faint moan. At least I knew I was headed in the right direction, and she was alive. I continued toward the sound, not thinking about what I might find.

"Amb—" I never got to finish. The ground beneath me gave away from the downpour, and I found myself in a combined slide and tumble down a steep embankment. Tree branches and ferns smacked me in the face as mud filled my ears and nose. Sheer terror took hold of me. I tried to partially open my mouth to scream, but nothing came out. I didn't dare open any further, fearing that I would inhale mud and suffocate.

After what seemed like an eternity, I finally stopped falling. As I lay on the hard, rocky ground, motionless, I took inventory of all my injuries. I felt every bruise and scrape from head to toe. At least I knew I wasn't paralyzed. I took a few minutes to catch my breath. It was so hard to breathe. I think I broke some ribs when I fell. I kept my eyes closed. It helped the throbbing headache, dizziness, and nausea.

I heard running water—not just a trickle like in the creek, but a powerful, continuous roar.

Again, I heard a faint moan. I opened my eyes and attempted to sit up. Oh! The whole world was moving. It felt like when I got beat up during my initiation into the group of my so-called friends.

I struggled to my feet and looked around. Through the flashes of lightning, I could see the embankment I fell down. It must have been one hundred feet or more! I was lucky to be alive and not critically injured!

The river was in front of me. I slowly bent down and dipped my hands into the water. Carefully, I scrubbed the mud from my face. The icy cold helped to clear my head, but it sure stung my scratches and abrasions.

I had to locate Amber and find a place for us to stay safe while the storm continued to rage.

"Help me," I heard a weak voice say. I could see the outline of a person approximately twenty feet away. As I stumbled closer, I saw Amber sitting on the ground with her back against a tree. Instantly, I could tell there was something wrong with her left leg. Her shin was abnormally bent, and there was blood on her ripped pant leg. She had been there for at least several hours.

"So now you're talking?" I asked as I bent down to check Amber's injuries. I didn't intend to sound sarcastic.

The hurt look on her face was from more than just her leg pain.

"I'm sorry," I apologized. "I didn't mean it like that."

"It's okay," she answered. "I'm sure I deserved that after the way I treated you last night."

"Have you been out here all night?" I asked as I continued to check for further injuries. So far, the broken leg appeared to be the worst of her problems.

"Most of it," she responded. "I waited until everyone was asleep, then I tiptoed out of the cabin."

"Why?" I asked. I had finished checking for other breaks and now looked into her eyes.

She didn't get a chance to answer. A bolt of lightning struck another tree. We had to find shelter and right now!

"This is gonna hurt," I warned her as I used some tree limbs and my shoelaces to splint her leg. Carefully, I picked her up and walked beside the river, looking for a place to wait out the storm.

With every step I took, I felt Amber wince in pain. *Please let me find shelter*, I silently prayed. From what I remembered about first aid last year in health class, I knew that hypothermia and shock could set in fast.

Up ahead, I could see a hollowed out overhang in the cliff. It sure wasn't perfect, but it would do. We were still in danger of being struck by lightning or hit by falling debris from the massive trees overhead.

As we approached the area, I did a quick look around to make sure there weren't any wild animals with the same idea of waiting out the storm. Fortunately, there weren't any.

I gently eased Amber to the ground. There really wasn't any way of making this more comfortable. With the storm's fury continuing and no end in sight, I knew I had to stay calm and get help quickly to prevent any life-threatening complications for Amber.

"I need to find something to get you warm," I told her.

"No," she weakly answered. "Please don't leave me. I don't know if I'll make it."

She looked so frail. I sensed her time on earth ticking by with each passing second. I looked her in the eyes and knew her life depended on me.

"I'll be right back," I said as my voice cracked. "I promise."

I didn't know anything about outdoor survival, but I was willing to do whatever it took to keep her alive. I couldn't lose another person I cared about.

CHAPTER 11

I covered Amber up with my jacket and left the overhang. There were a few branches on the ground that I propped against the opening to provide a protective shield. At least it would block some of the torrential rain and wind. As far as fire and food were concerned, that would take a miracle.

As I made my way along the river, I looked for anything I might be able to utilize. It was hard to see, though. It was only midmorning, but it seemed dark enough to be midnight. The periodic flashes of lightning were both a blessing and a curse. I briefly had some light to illuminate my way, but the power of the electricity and the accompanying thunder terrified me.

I walked for what seemed like hours, though I'm sure it was only minutes. I was drenched, tired, hungry, and weak. The thought of Amber alone and in need of medical attention prodded me on.

It was hard to breathe with my broken ribs, and I was eventually forced to take a break. As I sat on a rock huddled under some brush, the sound of the river began to lull me to sleep. I tried so hard to fight off the exhaustion. My eyelids felt so heavy, as if there were weights on them. Before I knew it, I was out.

A calm, somewhat familiar sounding voice coaxed me from my slumber. I opened my eyes and waited for the blurriness to wear off. At first I thought I was dreaming, but the bone-chilling cold from my wet clothes told me otherwise.

"Are you okay, Eli?" a man standing beside me asked. He looked to be around thirty years old, was clean shaven, had brown hair, and was remarkably dry for the amount of rain that continued to fall from the sky. I didn't recognize him, but I wasn't afraid.

"I think so," I replied, "but my friend's in bad shape. I think she's in shock and needs to get to the hospital."

"That was very brave and unselfish what you did for your friend. I'm proud of the man you've become."

"Thanks," I replied as I struggled to stand up. My head was still a bit fuzzy from my earlier fall, so I didn't quite understand what the man said. "Where'd you come from? I didn't know anyone else was out here in this storm."

"I used to come here often. It was where I would come to think and ask God for forgiveness for what I've done."

"It can't be any worse than what I've done," I said sadly. "I got stuck at kiddie prison for the summer, because I've been in so much trouble."

"I'm sure it was tough for your mother to make the decision to have you sent here."

"I know," I acknowledged. "She's had it rough since my brother died and my dad left when I was a kid."

"I'm sure he regretted that every day of his life."

"Yeah, I doubt it," I responded sarcastically. "By the way, what's your name?"

"It's Timothy Joel, but my friends call me TJ."

The rain, thunder, and lightning stopped, and there was now a ray of sunshine peaking down through the glistening branches. I could finally see the river and the surrounding area better. Something shiny near the river's edge caught my attention. As I walked closer, I saw what looked like a camouflaged backpack hidden behind a log and covered with overgrown ferns. Only the buckle gave away its location. Who knows how long it had been there or to whom it belonged.

"Hey, look what I found!" I yelled excitedly as I picked it up. I turned around, but TJ had disappeared.

"Weird! I must be hallucinating. Now I'm talking to myself!"

The backpack felt fairly heavy and was made of a waterproof material. I quickly unzipped it and said a silent plea that there would be something in there to help Amber. My prayer was answered! Not only were there dry matches and an instant fire log, but there was a heat-retaining blanket, some dry clothes, freeze dried foods, bottled water, and a first-aid kit!

Thank God! I pondered the odds of finding exactly what I needed when I needed it.

I hurried back to Amber as quickly as I could. Upon arrival, I realized her condition had deteriorated. She was shivering, pale, and lethargic. I had to act fast.

"Amber, it's me, Eli," I said as I pulled out the fire log, cleared a spot on the ground, and lit it. I was careful to make sure the smoke would vent out the entrance and not choke us.

"Are you able to take off your wet clothes and put these on?" I asked as I removed a hoodie and some zippered cargo pants from the backpack.

"I think so," she murmured as I held up the blanket to provide a makeshift changing room for her. She was able to change into the hoodie, but she stopped to rest before attempting the daunting task of changing her pants with a broken leg.

While she rested, I found some scissors in the first-aid kit. I figured I could cut her pants to make it easier for her to remove them. Then I could check the break to see how bad it was. I slowly took the splint off her leg and cut the side seams of her pants.

I tried hard to not show emotion when I pulled back the fabric covering her lower leg, but I couldn't hide my concern. The swollen, bruised tissue and the jagged piece of bone protruding from her shin made me shudder with empathy pain.

"It's bad, isn't it?" she asked with panic in her voice. Her eyes pleaded with me for a truthful answer.

"We'll be out of here as soon as they find us. Trevor had the entire camp out looking for you before breakfast. I'm sure it won't be long." I tried to sound confident and strong to hide my fear and insecurity. I had never seen an injury that severe.

"Here," I said as I handed her some pain pills and a small amount of water from the backpack. "Take these before you change the rest of your clothes."

"Thanks," she responded as she gratefully took what I offered her.

"I found some honey and crackers. Eat a bit, and get some energy." There were more substantial foods in the backpack, but I didn't want to chance having surgery delayed due to a full belly. I had made that mistake a few years before when I loaded up on ice cream and popsicles right before I was scheduled to have my tonsils removed.

Mom was furious and said that was supposed to be for after surgery. As Amber nibbled the snack, I searched through the medical supplies until I found what I needed.

"I don't mean to hurt you more," I forewarned as I carefully poured some antiseptic cleanser onto Amber's leg fracture. She closed her eyes and clenched her jaw and fists, trying to cope with the pain. Gently, I applied antibiotic ointment and a bandage to the area.

"Are you doing okay?" I asked as I prepared her for the hardest part.

"I'm hangin' in there," she answered with gritted teeth.

As efficiently as I could, I immobilized the area with the splint and ACE wrap I found in the first-aid kit. I could tell this was taking a toll on her. The sweat that had beaded up on her forehead now dripped down her face.

I then zipped off the lower section of the left pant leg and eased the dry clothing over the splint and dressing until it reached her knee. "Do you need any help?" I offered in a concerned rather than a romantic way.

"Thanks, but I think I can do it."

I again held up the blanket for a privacy curtain. My heart ached with helplessness while Amber moaned and cried out in pain. Getting dressed lying down was hard enough. Doing it with a compound fracture was almost impossible. At least the dry clothes belonged to a man and were big enough for her to wiggle into.

When she was finished, I tucked the blanket around her and pulled the hood over her wet hair. Thankfully, the fire had warmed Amber up enough to stop shivering.

"Thanks," she said, trying to hide her embarrassment. "I didn't mean to cause so much trouble."

"It was you that found my map with detailed escape plans, wasn't it?" I asked.

"Yes," she said sheepishly.

"I thought up a few different ways to escape, but this seemed like the one that you'd choose. I didn't remember the map's specifics until I heard you were missing. If I wouldn't have followed you, I wouldn't have found this." I then pulled the bracelet out of my pocket.

Tears welled up in her eyes as she realized what I held in my hand. As I reached over to fasten it around her wrist, I noticed large scars on the inner aspect of her lower arm. My eyes darted to her other arm where I could see similar marks extending from underneath her other bracelet.

Our eyes locked as a single tear cascaded down her cheek.

"What happened?" I softly asked, knowing exactly what she felt.

She took a long slow breath to calm her emotions. "Last year, my family and I were in a car accident. I was the only survivor."

"I'm so sorry," I replied. "I had no idea."

"That's not the worst part," she continued. "I was the driver. I had my learner's permit, and my parents offered to let me drive home from my State Gymnastics Meet. They were so proud of how well I did—near perfect scores on my beam, bar, and floor routines. I had driven lots of times before, but there wasn't any moonlight that night. A summer rainstorm hit during the competition, and we didn't know how slick the roads were." She paused to control the crack in her voice.

"We were talking about the competition and my upcoming plans for the regionals and nationals. The next thing I knew, we were spinning in circles across I-5 Southbound. The edge of the rear tire caught the gravel in the median, and we flipped over and over. I woke up in the ICU three days later. I had a severe concussion and needed surgery to repair the tendons and vessels in my wrists where the shattered windshield cut me. My grandparents broke the news that my parents and my sister were killed instantly. Jade would've turned ten today."

We sat in silence for a few minutes, watching the flames of the fire.

"Is that why you haven't been talking, why you tried to run away today?" I asked quietly.

"Yeah," she answered. "I hadn't said a word since the day of the accident. My grandparents sent me here after the therapists, pastors, and grief counselors were unable to help. There were a few times I tried to reopen my scars with a kitchen knife. I figured I didn't deserve to still be here. I wanted to either be with them or continue to feel the pain, remind me they're gone because of me."

"Is that why you wear the bracelets?" I wondered.

"My grandparents had them made for me. One is for my parents, and the other is for my sister. They said they would remind me that my family is still with me. I think they made them to prevent me from cutting myself again."

"What does your other bracelet say?" I asked.

"My loving parents are my guardian angels."

I reached over and took her hand in mine. "I'm glad you're here," I managed to say. My throat was so tight from choking back my tears during her heart-wrenching story. I never thought I would ever meet someone with an equally painful past.

"Me, too," she responded as she leaned her head onto my shoulder and drifted off to sleep. Apparently, the medication had eased the pain in her leg. I hoped talking had helped lessen the pain in her soul.

CHAPTER 12

I don't know how long we rested by the warmth of the fire. A sound in the distance woke me from my nap. Amber continued to sleep, but it looked like she was getting worse. She was now breathing faster, and the rapid pulse on her inner wrist could barely be felt. I was angry at myself for falling asleep and not keeping better watch over Amber. Gently, I eased her to a lying position and crept to the opening of our shelter. The sunlight streamed in as I pushed away the door of branches. I strained to hear extra noises over the rushing water of the river.

"Amber!" "Eli!" Voices were calling our names in the distance and sounded like they were getting closer.

"Help us!" I yelled back. "Over here!"

Within a matter of seconds, I saw Junior and the guys from my cabin rounding the bend. I could see a look of relief on Junior's face as he sprinted over to me.

"Thank God you're safe!" he said. "Where's Amber?"

"She's in here. Please help her!" I pleaded. "She broke her leg, and it's bad!"

My friends gathered around and told me how glad they were to find us alive. From what they heard over the emergency radio, that was the worst storm the area had experienced in over ten years. All I could do was watch helplessly as Junior knelt down beside Amber to check on her condition. I knew things were really bad when he looked up at us and said, "Boys, I need you to say a prayer for Amber while I call for the chopper."

As Junior radioed our location to the guard station, I gathered my group in a circle and had everyone bow their heads. "Lord," I began. "I know I've been a horrible person. I've done some awful things, and I'm really sorry. I don't deserve to ask any favors from you, but it's for Amber. Please let her get better. She deserves a second chance at life. I promise to be a better person and do whatever it is you want me to do. Just please, help her. Amen."

My friends said "Amen" with me then gave me pats on the back and words of encouragement. It was at that point that I realized what true friendship was. My friends back home would never have come looking for me, let alone pray with me.

Several minutes later, I heard the eerily familiar *whump, whump, whump* of the blades as the air ambulance appeared over the tree tops and descended onto the rocky area by the river. The pilot barely had enough room between the side of the cliff and the trees across the river, but he managed to set the chopper on the ground without any problems. Luck or a higher power was on his side that day.

As soon as it was safe to disembark, two flight nurses hurried to the shelter with their stretcher and supplies. They quickly and methodically checked Amber over and asked me questions about how long she had been this way, when she last ate or drank, and what medication she had taken. While they asked questions, they started an IV and got her loaded onto the stretcher.

Before I could ask if Amber would be okay, she was wheeled past me toward the helicopter. Seeing the concern on my face, the nurses stopped briefly. Amber looked so frail, pale, and weak. She was unconscious and unaware of what was happening.

"You did a great job today!" the senior flight nurse said to me. "What you did for her probably saved her life. She can still hear you if you want to quickly say something to her."

I timidly approached and took her hand in mine. "Please don't leave me, Amber," I whispered to her. "I need you." I thought I saw her eyelids flutter, but there wasn't time to wait for a response. The flight nurses had to get her to the hospital before her condition got worse. They rolled her into the cargo area, secured her stretcher inside the chopper, and closed the door.

As they ascended toward the sky, I kept having flashbacks of when I was four. I never saw Ian again after he was taken to the hospital in the helicopter. *What if I never see Amber again? What if this happened because of my map?* The possibility of her dying and of it being my fault made my gut churn. Without warning, I turned to a nearby bush and brought up sour bile from my stomach.

Junior had my friends put out the fire and pack up the items in the shelter while he gave me a few minutes to process the events of the last ten hours.

When I had regained control of myself, Junior approached me. He quietly stood by me while I attempted to explain what happened. "I'm so sorry," I managed to say through my tears. "It was my fault Amber ran away. She found the map I sketched for my own escape. I never meant for anyone to get hurt, especially Amber. I'd take it all back if I could."

After I had finished unloading my guilty conscience to Junior, the most unexpected thing happened. He hugged me. Not a "weird, awkward, get away from me" kind of hug but a reassuring "been there, done that" and "you'll get through this" kind of hug. Except for when Aunt Bea hugged me when I was a kid, I never let anyone get that close to me. Ever since Ian died, I had pushed everyone away—including Mom. The ironic thing is that hug was just what I needed.

"Come back to the cabin, and change into some dry clothes before you go to the hospital. You need to have your ribs checked out. I had the cook put some food in the oven for you," Junior said as he guided me and the rest of my friends along the river toward the road.

As we trudged up the embankment to the road that took us back to the camp, I began to feel every scrape, bruise, and break. With each step, I felt weaker and had more trouble breathing. I had forgotten about my injuries while I was taking care of Amber. They now reminded me with a vengeance, but I didn't dare complain. My pain was nothing compared to what Amber had endured.

When we got back, Trevor met us at the main gate. "Thank God you're both alive! Matt will help you to your cabin, and I'll get you some dinner."

"I'm so sorry, Trevor," I managed to respond. "I didn't mean for Amber to get hurt. She found the map I drew to escape from here. She told me what happened to her family. I didn't mean to add to her pain." My head hung in shame, and I couldn't bear to look him in the eyes. I was sure he would tack on extra time to my sentence, but I deserved it.

"She talked?" Trevor asked. "You must have earned her trust and helped her start the recovery process. What you don't know is she tried to escape from other facilities before. Your map didn't cause what happened today."

"Thanks," I said as I turned and headed toward the Courage cabin.

Matt walked beside me and helped me up the steps into the cabin. "I'm glad you're okay," he stated. "You're like family to me."

I didn't know how to respond, so I just nodded my appreciation to Matt.

I took a hot shower and scrubbed the mud from my entire body. As the water washed away the layers of grime, I felt like my anger and hatred were also going down the drain.

By the time I was dried off and dressed, Trevor had arrived with my plate of food. Unlike the last time food was brought to me, I ate it without hesistation. I could only eat a little, though. I still wasn't feeling well.

"Are you ready to go?" Trevor asked.

"Can Matt go with us?" I asked, strangely overcome with brotherly affection. I wondered what Ian would have been like. *Would he have been like Matt?*

"Of course," he replied. "We'll probably see Bo there. We got a call earlier today that his girlfriend Jasmine was in labor. I had Gabe drive Bo to the hospital to be with her."

I unloaded the first-aid kit and the survival gear from the backpack I'd found and put my Bible, a pencil, and some paper in. I figured I might as well take something to do, in case I got bored waiting in the ER.

The drive back to town was almost as stressful as the drive to New Beginnings Camp. I was so worried about Amber. There had been no news about her condition since she was flown to the hospital. It was hard to believe that less than a week had passed since we met. I couldn't imagine never having known her or what I would do without her.

When we arrived at Holy Waters Community Hospital, I convinced Trevor to take me to see Amber before I had my own injuries checked out. We met Amber's grandparents in the ICU waiting room and received some great news. She had gone straight to surgery, and the doctors were hopeful she would fully recover. She was also treated fast enough to keep her shock from getting worse. It was likely she'd be in the hospital for several days, but she was strong-willed enough to bounce back quicker.

Amber's grandparents hugged me, grateful for what I had done to help their only grandchild. The car accident the previous year had taken their only son and other granddaughter. Her grandma then briefly went to the nurses' station and came back with a twinkle in her eye.

"Amber is resting, but you can go see her for a few minutes before visiting hours are over. I told a white lie, though," she said with a mischievous grin on her face. "Only family can visit, so I told the nurses you were her fiancé."

"Oh," I stammered, my face flushed from embarrassment. "I'll be right back."

I tiptoed into Amber's wall-free room, not wanting to wake her if she was asleep. The number of monitors, machines, and tubes attached to her frail body was overwhelming. Her leg was covered in bandages and ice packs. She appeared to sleep, so I quietly approached her bed and sat in the chair. She looked more comfortable than she did in the shelter, but she sure had a long recovery ahead of her.

As I reached over and placed my hand on hers, she turned toward me and opened her eyes. "Hi," I said, completely caught off guard.

"Hi," she weakly answered. "I hope I didn't get you into trouble."

"No. I think things will be okay back at camp," I reassured her.

"Thanks for what you did. I'm sorry for being mean to you last night at the amphitheater."

"Did I do something to make you mad?" I asked, truly wondering what I did to upset her.

She thought for a minute, trying to find the words to explain her behavior. "When you nearly fell at the ropes course yesterday, I realized how close you were to dying. After my car accident, I promised myself I wouldn't get attached to anyone. I broke my rule this week when I met you."

"Me too," I responded, knowing I had found my soul mate. The nurse came in and said visiting hours were over. I needed to let her rest. "I'll call to check on you tomorrow. I have to go back with Trevor tonight."

"Okay." She smiled and drifted off to sleep.

I bent over to kiss her forehead. "Good night, and may God's angels watch over you," I whispered, repeating what Mom used to say at bedtime when I was a child.

I tiptoed back out of the room, feeling like I was floating on air.

CHAPTER 13

I returned to the waiting room and told Trevor I was ready to have my injuries checked out. While I was visiting Amber, he was finally able to call Mom and inform her about what happened. Apparently, the storm had knocked out power and phone service to our town for most of the day. She was nearly hysterical when she found out about the incident, but Trevor was able to calm her down and reassure her I was safe. He said my mom would be meeting us downstairs in the ER.

As we got on the elevator to go downstairs, we ran into Bo. He had just come from the Mother-and-Baby Unit and was on his way to visit Amber.

"Hey, Bo," I said to him. "Amber is gonna be okay. She's asleep right now, but I'll call her tomorrow and tell her you stopped by. How's Jasmine doing?"

"We have a girl!" he beamed. "She was born earlier this afternoon. We named her McKenzie after the area that changed my life."

"I'm so proud of you," Trevor said as he patted him on the shoulder.

"Do you want to see her?" Bo asked.

"We'd love to," I answered, again forgetting about my aches and pains. I didn't want to miss my first opportunity to see a new baby.

We followed Bo back onto the elevator and ascended to the next floor. "Jasmine had a long night and needed some rest, so Kenzie is being watched by the nurses for a while," he explained as he motioned us to a viewing area.

We stood outside the nursery and looked through the window as Bo washed his hands and donned a gown. With help from a nurse, he bent down over a bassinet and picked up a small bundle wrapped in a pink blanket. As he turned around and approached the window, Trevor, Matt, and I all gasped. She was so tiny, beautiful, and perfect all at the same time! Her innocence and an entire lifetime ahead of her sparked my hope in a new start for me.

"Congratulations!" we whispered to Bo so we didn't wake the baby.

Bo carefully put the newborn back before she became fussy, and he came out to talk with us.

"Is it all right if I stay with Jasmine and Kenzie?" Bo asked Trevor. "I still have some time left on my sentence, but I can't bear the thought of leaving them right now."

"From what I've seen," responded Trevor, "I think Judge Mosaron will be able to shorten your sentence as long as you have a safe, stable place to go after leaving New Beginnings Camp."

"Yes, sir!" he exclaimed.

"I'm happy for you," I told Bo before he hurried back to check on his girlfriend.

Trevor and I returned to the elevator and descended to the first floor. I checked in at admitting, informed the triage nurse about my symptoms, and was taken back for an evaluation within minutes. I asked to have Trevor and Matt remain with me. I still wasn't comfortable enough with doctors, nurses, and hospitals to be there by myself. I figured I had PTSD from Ian's drowning and attempted resuscitation. The staff told me they would bring my mom back as soon as she arrived.

After I had changed into a gown, a doctor came in to evaluate me. He listened to my heart, lungs, and belly and looked into my eyes, nose, and ears. After speaking with a nurse, he told me I was to have labs drawn then be transported to the x-ray department for some scans.

The nurse quickly returned, drew the blood, and started an IV. She had just finished when the radiology staff arrived with the wheelchair to whisk me off for the tests. *Wow! Things sure move fast around here!*

"I'll see you in a bit," Trevor called to me as I was rushed down the hall. Matt was right behind. He intended to keep his promise to stay with me.

Trevor later told me what happened while I was gone. He sat down in a chair near the ER bed and had waited approximately ten minutes when he heard a commotion nearby. His chair was partially hidden by a privacy curtain, and the bright overhead light had been dimmed while I was away.

He heard the frantic voice of a woman begging the staff to tell her where I was and what was wrong with me. "Please!" she said between sobs. "I can't lose my son! He's all I have left!"

"Ma'am," the nurse addressed her. "We're doing everything we can to find out what is wrong with your son and get him the treatment he needs. Please have a seat, and we'll update you as soon as we know anything."

Trevor took that verbal cue and stood up from the chair as the nurse hurried from the room. The sound of movement caused Mom to turn toward Trevor. He didn't say anything as she slowly approached him.

Mom gasped and stopped in disbelief, absolutely stunned by the figure standing before her.

"Hello, Elizabeth," Trevor addressed her. "I'm glad you're here."

"TJ?" she stammered. From across the room and with shadows concealing his identity, Trevor looked just like her husband—wrinkled clothing, uncombed hair, beard stubble. She could have sworn it was twelve years earlier, both of them together in a hospital, waiting for news about their son Ian.

"No," he replied as he stepped into the light. "It's Trevor, TJ's father."

"But TJ always told me his dad was dead," Mom said slowly as she tried to put the pieces together.

"That doesn't surprise me. It's easier for a kid to tell his friends that his dad is dead than to tell them that he's in prison."

"But you never called or tried to make contact with us. Why?" she questioned with anger in her voice.

"You might want to sit down for this," Trevor said as he motioned Mom over to the chair. "My ex-wife Charlotte never gave me any news on TJ or his sister Alexis. She never forgave me for what I did. My kids spent their entire teenage years without a father. I was still in prison when I heard Alexis and her husband were killed in a plane crash. Charlie raised Ali's son Matt from the time he was a baby until he was in preschool.

"I had just been released from prison and started my life over at New Beginnings Camp when I was informed Charlie had died from a heart attack. Her sister, Bea, would have taken care of Matt, but she already had her hands full helping take care of his cousin. With permission from Judge Mosaron, I brought Matt to the camp and raised him. At the time, Bea felt like Eli wasn't ready to hear about his other family. She died before I could reach out to Eli and tell him the truth about his father. With Bea's passing, all ways of contacting Eli or you were lost.

"It was just last week that I received a call from the judge and realized who our new camper was. I haven't told him yet. I thought he should be told when we're all together."

"Together for what?" I asked as I was wheeled back into the room from the radiology department. Matt helped me out of the wheelchair so I could greet Mom with a hug and a kiss on the cheek. She seemed shaken up, but the doctor came back in before they could answer my question.

"Young man," the doctor said, "your head CT looked okay. You only have a mild concussion. Unfortunately though, you have broken ribs that have caused other injuries. Your spleen has a puncture and is leaking fluid into your abdomen. The left lung is partially collapsed and needs to be repaired. You're lucky to be alive. Injuries like those are critical when they're not caught in time. The OR is being prepped, and the nurse is on her way with the consent form. I'll see you in there."

I crawled back onto the ER bed, feeling weaker than I ever had. Each breath became more labored, and my body looked like I was pregnant.

"We'll talk about things after you're feeling better. Right now, we need to focus on getting you well."

"Trevor's right," Mom agreed with a shaky voice. "I love you, Eli. I hope someday you can forgive me for calling the police. I couldn't see any other way of saving you from a crime-filled life."

"It's okay, Mom," I said as I put my hand on hers. "I'm not mad. I actually met some people I consider real friends." I glanced up and smiled at Trevor and Matt.

"If you don't mind," Trevor said, "I would like to say a prayer before you go into surgery."

"I'd like that," Mom said as she reached out to Trevor's outstretched hand.

When all four of us had our hands joined, we closed our eyes and bowed our heads. "Lord," Trevor began. "We ask that you be with Eli as he undergoes surgery. Guide the surgeons' hands as they repair his body. Give Eli the strength to recover from his injuries and to restore his faith in you. Show him the way back to the path you intend for him to follow. This we ask in Jesus' name. Amen."

"Amen," we repeated after Trevor.

I looked up to see Mom wipe tears from her eyes. "I'll be okay," I told her.

The gurney that would take me to the OR arrived just then. I had enough time to shake hands with Trevor and Matt and give Mom a quick hug. I was transferred onto the gurney by the OR staff while the nurse had Mom sign my consent for surgery. With a quick "Bye," I was whisked down the corridor and onto another elevator that went to the OR floor. Matt wasn't allowed to follow any further. As the elevator door closed, I saw him go back in the direction of the ER.

I closed my eyes as the elevator rose. I felt so alone and scared; emotions I would never have admitted to at home. Strange things had happened in the past few days. I hoped Trevor was right, and there was someone up above who continued to watch over me.

CHAPTER 14

I was transported to the pre-op department to briefly meet with the anesthesiologist before surgery. He quickly asked me some questions about my medical history before the nurses wheeled me into the OR. The staff immediately transferred me onto the surgical table and attached several monitors to my body. I was glad they hurried; it was so hard to breathe.

I could hear the different beeps from the monitors as the anesthesiologist placed the mask over my nose and mouth. In the distance, I saw the surgeons being assisted into their gowns and sterile gloves. I tried so hard to keep my eyes open, but I couldn't fight the effects of the pungent anesthetic gas. It was such a surreal feeling to lose total control and be completely dependent on the surgeons to fix me and the anesthesiologist to keep me unaware of anything that was going on.

The most unexplainable thing happened while I was under the anesthesia. A few minutes into the operation, I sat up and walked away from the OR table. Halfway across the OR, I looked down to find myself in a hospital gown—no evidence I just had surgery. As I turned around to see what had happened, I realized my body was still on the table. The surgeons were working as hard as they could to repair my spleen, clean out the excess fluid from my abdomen, and sew me back together. Another doctor arrived and was shoving a tube into my side to re-expand my left lung. One nurse was doing chest compressions while another started a second IV line. The anesthesiologist was at the head of the bed, pushing medication through the lines and adjusting the ventilator.

More and more people rushed into the OR. Some brought units of blood for transfusions while others brought supplies and assisted the other staff. Everyone seemed to have a job, and they worked together like an efficient machine.

I made my way over to the side of the room. I couldn't help but wonder, *Am I alive, or am I dead?*

As I watched the scene unfold, a gentle, familiar voice next to me said, "Don't be afraid. You will be okay, no matter which way things turn out."

I looked to my right and saw the man from the river bank standing beside me. He looked just like he had the last time I saw him. "TJ!" I exclaimed, surprised to see him again. "Am I dead?"

"Yes and no," he replied. "The doctors and nurses are keeping your body alive. You're having what is sometimes called an out-of-body experience. I don't know if you'll make it through surgery or not. It's not up to me. Whether you stay here or move on will depend on the choices you've made in the past."

"You mean like whether I've been bad or good?" I asked, really starting to get worried. I hadn't been the best person, but I certainly wasn't the worst.

"No," he calmly answered, looking at me with comforting eyes. "There is but one way that determines where you go after you leave this world. It involves courage, wisdom, faith, and hope. It is to trust that Jesus loved us so much he died to save us from our sins, to ask him for forgiveness for what we've done in the past, and to walk in the path that brings glory to his name."

I was stunned! Not only did he name off all the cabins at the camp, but he said somebody loved me so much that he actually died for me! Me!

I looked over at the OR table again. There didn't seem to be as much activity as there was just a moment ago. *What does that mean?*

When I looked back to ask TJ what was happening, he was gone. I then became aware I was no longer standing along the wall. I was lying on the OR table; surgery had just finished. *I survived!* I felt the anesthesiologist take the tube out of my throat. The first breath was so painful, especially when I coughed. The searing pain in my upper abdomen was far more than what I had expected.

I was still unable to open my eyes while I was moved off the OR table onto a gurney. As I was taken down the hall to the recovery room, the motion of the gurney made my stomach feel like I was on a roller coaster. Just when I felt like throwing up, the movement stopped.

The voices were muffled, but I could pick up bits and pieces of the report the anesthesiologist gave to the nurse in the recovery room. I definitely heard the words *coded* and *chest compressions* as I drifted back to sleep.

I don't know how long I was unconscious in the recovery room. When I woke, I could tell by the clock on the wall it was 11:30.

"What day is it?" I asked the nurse standing beside my bed, writing in my chart. I was disoriented and couldn't tell if it was morning or night.

"It's Friday night," the brunette in her late thirties answered. "How is your pain?"

"I feel awful. Can I have some pain medicine?" I moaned.

"Sure," she said as she attached a syringe to my IV line and pushed some medication through the adapter. "This will help your pain." She then hooked a machine up to my IV line and handed me a controller. "The machine will give you a continuous small amount of medicine in your IV, but you can also push the button for a dose when it gets really bad."

"I won't get too loaded, will I?" I asked, concerned about accidentally overdosing myself.

"No," she reassured me. "It's preprogrammed and won't give you any more after the limits are reached. Don't worry though, it will reset when the lockout time is complete. Let's get you transferred over to the ICU. You'll be spending the night in there for observation. You definitely had a guardian angel watching over you today."

"Yeah, I sure did." I smiled as I recalled the conversation I had with TJ in the OR. I was still unsure if it was real or not.

Knowing I was headed to the ICU gave me hope of seeing Amber again.

As I was wheeled out of the recovery room, the nurse briefly paused in the hall with the gurney. Mom, Trevor, and Matt rushed to my side to see how I was.

"Hi," I managed to say through a hoarse voice and a painful grimace. I could tell Mom had been crying; her eyes were puffy and red. Trevor and Matt both looked worried and tired.

"I thought I had lost you," Mom said as she stifled a sob. "I heard them call a code blue and saw doctors and nurses running down the hall toward the OR." She bent over the gurney and gave me a gentle hug and a kiss on the cheek. "You're all I have left in this world," she expressed in a choked-up voice as she fluffed my hair with her fingers.

Trevor reached over and placed his hand on Mom's shoulder to let her know she wasn't alone. "God was sure watching over you tonight, Eli," he said. "We'll be right here in the waiting room until visiting hours start in the morning," he declared as he gave my hand a squeeze of encouragement.

Matt then nervously approached the gurney as Mom and Trevor stepped aside. "I'm glad you're okay," he said as he fist-bumped mine.

"I'm sorry," the nurse interrupted, "but we really need to get him settled into the ICU for the night. You can visit him in the morning."

As we resumed our trek down the hall toward the ICU, I couldn't help but reflect on the events of the day. It had been one of the longest days of my life. Not only did it affect my outlook on life, but it changed my soul. Ever since Ian died and Dad left, I had built a wall around myself. I never wanted to feel that kind of pain or loss again. If I didn't care about people, then I could prevent those horrible feelings. Nearly losing Amber today made me realize I was wrong. I needed to love and be loved. I now understood people cared about me, and I had a purpose in life.

My gurney was wheeled head-first into the bay with the number 7 above it. Several nurses greeted me and hooked me up to numerous monitors and machines.

I was so tired, but I managed to keep my eyes open long enough to peer through the open curtain near the foot of my bed. I just had to see Amber before I could sleep. The nurses' station was directly across from me. As I glanced around the circular unit, I saw the location I visited her in that afternoon. Inside, Amber was asleep in the bed. She looked so peaceful and not as weak as the last time I saw her.

The clock on my wall indicated it was midnight. A new day and a new chapter in my life was about to start. No matter how hard I tried to stay awake, wondering what the next day would bring, the quiet murmurs of the nurses and the rhythmic beeping of the monitors lulled me to sleep.

CHAPTER 15

I awakened to the sounds of shift change in the ICU. There were nurses, doctors, therapists, and other staff members all jockeying for position at the central nurses' station. Patients were being transported to specialized departments for tests and scans, while others were transferred to other floors and units. I could hear the cries from family members of the patient in the bay next to mine—an elderly man who suffered a massive stroke the previous day and was just taken off life support.

As I stared up at the ceiling, I thought about how ironic life can be. Just the day before I saw a brand-new baby beginning life. The man on the other side of the curtain was about to leave his behind.

An experienced radiology tech and my "way too chipper for this time of the morning" nurse interrupted my thoughts as they entered my room with a wheelchair.

"You're going to get abdominal and chest x-rays. We'll transfer you to the surgical floor if those look okay," my nurse informed me as she helped the tech move me into the wheelchair with my IV and various tubes and drains. "You'll still be hospitalized until tomorrow, but the drainage tubes will be removed later today if the x-rays this afternoon are stable." I pushed the button on my pain pump, hoping to take away the searing pain triggered by being up for the first time since surgery. I hurt from head to toe. As I sat waiting for the tech to get my chart from the desk, I saw my reflection in the window. The realization of just how bad I looked made me wince.

Now that's sexy! I sarcastically remarked to myself as I took in the whole picture—the scrapes and bruises to my face, the pee bag attached to my leg, the grenade-shaped drain with pink fluid pinned to my gown, the thick tubing inserted into my left lung connected to a drainage system, and the thigh-high white stockings to prevent blood clots in my legs.

My self-conscious distress soon disappeared. As I was wheeled slowly past Amber's bay, I was surprised to hear her giggling and visiting with her grandparents. Even though she still appeared worn-out and painful from her ordeal, she had a glow and energy that she didn't have before. When she glanced up and realized I was in the hall, she waved and called out a heart-felt "thank you" to me. I nodded and gave a shy smile as my wheelchair continued down the hall.

As we left the ICU and headed toward the radiology department, I was able to look around and get the layout of the hospital. When we passed the chapel, I caught a glimpse of Mom, Trevor, and Matt sitting in the pews. They looked tired, but there was also a look of relief on their faces.

The radiology tech noticed I craned my head around to look into the chapel as we passed. "There are two important things I've learned over the years," he said behind me as he pushed the wheelchair. "Number one, it's never too late to change and make things right. You decide how your life will turn out. And number two, a doctor once taught me that every day is a good day. Always try to see the good in any situation. I hope you find what you're looking for. You seem like a nice young man."

"Thanks," I responded, not knowing what else to say. *If a complete stranger thinks I have potential, maybe I do.* I decided I would come back to the chapel sometime before I was discharged. Maybe I had found what I was looking for.

When I returned to the ICU, I noticed the housekeeping staff cleaning Amber's empty room. I started to panic. "Where's Amber?" I asked the charge nurse behind the desk.

She could see the worry and distress on my face. The staff knew the story of our rescue in the woods. "It's okay. Amber was just transferred to the surgical floor. I'm sure you won't be far behind," she said with a reassuring smile.

"Thanks," I replied with relief. The radiology tech and my nurse helped get me settled back into bed just as Mom, Trevor, and Matt entered.

"I'll be back as soon as I have your x-ray results and orders from your doctor," my nurse said.

Mom immediately came over and gave me a hug. "How are you doing, sweetie?" she asked. It had been years since she had called me that. I chuckled as I remembered the day I stuffed a whole roll of sweet tarts in my mouth on a dare and earned myself the nickname. Mom said my expression was priceless.

"I'm okay," I answered. "Amber was already moved to another floor. I should be able to go too if my test results are good."

"Here's your backpack in case you need something out of it," Trevor said as he handed me the bag I found out by the river.

"I packed something else for you," Matt said with a grin. "I heard chocolate makes everything better, so I hope it works! The cook helped me make it."

"Thanks, guys," I said as I eagerly opened the backpack to find what treasure was hidden inside. I was pleased to find a homemade brownie Matt hid right before we left camp for the hospital.

As I chomped down on the treat from my friend, something caught my eye. I reached into the backpack and pulled out a sealed envelope. In my haste to unpack the survival gear, first-aid kit, and dry clothes, I didn't see the inner pocket that held an envelope. I nearly choked on my brownie as I turned the envelope over and read who it was addressed to—Elizabeth, Eli, and Trevor.

I took a sip of water from my bedside table as my visitors looked on with curiosity. Slowly, I opened the envelope and discovered there were three folded pieces of paper inside it. As I took them out, I realized each paper was a personalized letter.

"What are those?" Mom asked as I held out the letters addressed to her and Trevor.

"I'm not sure," I said in an unsteady voice, "but I think they're from someone we know."

Mom and Trevor suddenly turned white as ghosts. They quickly found chairs to sit in before they fell over. Matt and I were completely confused as to what was going on.

"Who wants to go first?" I asked as we each held our letters in our shaking hands.

"I will," Trevor said as he slowly opened the handwritten letter and began to read it aloud.

Dear Dad,

I'm sorry I never got a chance to really know you. For the longest time, I was so angry at you for what you did. I know you never meant to hurt Mom, Alexis, or me, and the decision to rob a bank was your attempt at making a better life for us. I forgive you.

I too tried to be a good man, but I failed. I let myself become distracted, and in the process, I lost my entire family. I wanted you to know I'm so sorry I never tried to reconnect with you as I was growing up. I know Mom never forgave you or kept in touch, but Aunt Bea's promise to keep a watchful eye over all the kids gave me hope.

I wanted you to know I did become very successful in my career as an architect. I hope you found the donation of New Beginnings Camp to be beneficial. My goal was to create a facility to put kids back on the right path and restore their faith in life and God. I hope to see you someday to share what we've learned and to start over.

Your son,
TJ

If it weren't for Trevor's sniffling and the beeping of the monitors, you could've heard a pin drop. Our mouths hung open as the reality of the letter sunk in, except for Matt, who was still trying to figure out what just happened.

"So what did that mean?" Matt asked Trevor.

"Well," he said as he tried to relay the information to Mom, Matt, and me. "It appears that the anonymous donor of the land, buildings, and money to the camp was TJ. When I was released from prison, I had nowhere to go. Judge Mosaron handed me an envelope that contained keys and an address. Inside, an unsigned note said I was to go to the location to start over and do something good for others who were struggling to change. I was in absolute disbelief when I arrived at the destination. I thought someone had made a mistake. An attorney met me at camp, handed me the deed, and assured me it was mine.

"When Junior was released the following week, I asked him to help me develop a program to keep kids from making the same mistakes we did. We enrolled the first several campers within a few months and have been growing ever since.

"You and TJ were married," Trevor said as he looked at Mom, "so that makes me grandpa to both Matt and Eli. You boys are cousins."

Matt and I looked at each other in disbelief.

"Is this what I heard you and Mom talking about?" I asked, still dumbstruck by the news I had an extended family.

"Yes," Mom confirmed. "I just found out last night."

"Read your letter," I requested, wondering what other bombshells would be dropped.

Mom took a slow deep breath, trying to calm her nerves enough to read her letter.

My Dearest Liz,

Please forgive me for leaving you alone to cope with the loss of Ian and to be both mother and father to Eli. I could hardly take care of myself, let alone a family. My grief and guilt were unbearable, and I thought you would both be better off without me.

I drifted around for a few months and ended up at a mission after I hit rock-bottom. There, I met a minister who taught me about Jesus and true forgiveness. I was able to pull myself together soon after that and moved to Portland for a job at a prominent architecture firm. I worked hard to earn contracts with several international clients, but I knew there was something missing in my life—you.

I never meant to hurt you. You will always be the love of my life. I hope you'll forgive me someday and will agree to meet me for dinner or coffee. Without you, I have nothing. Everything I have I give to you and Eli. I will spend the rest of my life trying to win you back.

Always and forever yours,
TJ

Mom had a tear roll down her cheek as she attempted to hide her heartbreak. She had the "why didn't he come back" expression on her face.

I was next. Everyone looked at me holding my letter. What would it say? The anticipation was written on their faces. I could barely open the paper because my hands shook so much. My mouth was so dry, and my throat felt so tight I didn't know if any words would come out. I thought the pounding of my heart could be heard throughout the ICU. I took a small sip of water from the cup on my bedside table and began to read.

Dear Eli,

I want to begin by telling you how much I regret what happened. You were not to blame for anything. I should've been a better father that awful winter day and the years that followed. I was wrong to have left you and your mother. For that, I will never forgive myself.

I heard from Aunt Bea last month that you fell out of a tree. I was so worried when I got her letter. The thought of losing you, my only remaining child, nearly broke my heart. I was relieved to hear there were no major injuries.

As soon as I finish one more project, I plan to come home and give you and your mom the lives you deserve. I hope you'll be able to forgive me and be my little boy again. I love you very much.

Hugs and kisses,
Dad

I looked at Mom, Trevor, and Matt with confusion and emptiness. The letters were written when I was a boy, but that was years ago. *Where's Dad now?* The answer slowly dawned on me—the man at the river, the man in the OR. That was TJ, my dad, which meant he was dead!

Trevor saw the realization of the truth cast a shadow over my face. "I'm so sorry," he said. "Right before I was released from prison, I received word TJ had died. He went on a hike along the McKenzie River and jumped in to rescue some teens that got stranded on a log in the middle of some rapids. He made it out to them and back to the shore twice, but on his way back to shore with the third teen, he could no longer fight the current. He pushed the girl to the edge with his last bit of strength. He was a hero that day. His body was found later that evening. When I was released from prison, I was given a box with his ashes. I never knew about the backpack or the letters inside. He must have tossed it in the bushes before he jumped in to save the teens."

Trevor continued to fill in the gaps of our family history, "While I was in prison, Bea would send me a letter several times each year to let me know how Alexis and TJ were doing. She would see them occasionally when her sister took them to visit. Charlie refused to keep me in the loop, didn't want me to be a bad influence on our kids. She said she didn't want me to contact them until they were adults and able to decide for themselves if they wanted me in their lives.

"After Ali and TJ had grown up and started their own lives, I tried to reach out and contact them. They weren't quite ready to forgive me, though. So Bea would send me an update about my kids and grandchildren every few months.

"I was very sad to hear about the circumstances that led to TJ's leaving. I know neither of you knew about me," Trevor said as he addressed Mom and me, "but I too felt the ache and loss of Ian. I know what it's like to lose a child and should never have let you go through that by yourselves.

"Bea continued to send the updates even after I got out of prison and started New Beginnings Camp. The letters stopped about eight years ago, though. I assumed you found out about me and didn't want anything to do with me either. I didn't find out about Bea's stroke and death until recently.

"Last week, when Judge Mosaron contacted me to tell me about whom my new arrival would be, I was in disbelief. I didn't want to overload any of you with family drama though, so I chose to wait until you were both together. I do hope we can get to know each other. It gets pretty lonely to not have many family members."

As we sat there in stunned silence looking at each other, we had no idea what to say. Fortunately, we didn't have to. My nurse came in just then to inform me my test results looked good, and I was being transferred to another floor.

I felt relieved I was stable and physically healing. What I had trouble processing was how I would deal with the life-altering information I just received. For the second time in less than a week, I experienced betrayal, hurt, and confusion. *Who does that to a sixteen-year-old?* I just wanted to go back to that awful winter day when I was a kid, to prevent Ian's accident and have a normal childhood where I didn't feel like part of my life was missing.

CHAPTER 16

After my visitors left, my nurse got me prepared for my move to the surgical floor. As she took my vital signs and calculated my fluid totals for the shift, I could see her glance at me with a concerned look. When she completed her charting and had my belongings packed, she pulled the chair up next to my bed and sat down. She was in her midtwenties and hadn't yet developed the acquired manner of remaining emotionally detached from her patients and their situations.

"The past few days have been pretty crappy for you, huh?" she asked. Her demeanor surprised me but made me feel more at ease. The radiology tech was the only other staff member I felt comfortable with. They treated me like a person rather than just a patient with a problem.

"No doubt," I replied. "I just wanna get outta here and go home."

"Where's home?" she inquired.

"I thought I knew," I said with a sigh.

"I didn't mean to overhear the conversation between you and your family," she revealed. "I was sitting at my cubicle charting and overhead everything. Don't worry. I won't say anything to anyone. Do you want to talk about it?"

I sat there for a minute, trying to decide what to say. Without even thinking, I opened my mouth and asked, "Do you believe in miracles?"

A slight smile formed on my nurse's face, and she said, "I see miracles happen every day. You'll make it through this, and you'll become a stronger person because of what you've dealt with."

"Thanks," I responded. It had been a long time since I had a glimmer of hope for a better future.

I climbed into the wheelchair and was transported to the surgical floor by my nurse and an assistant. It was quite a feat trying to keep all of my tubes, drains, and the IV pole straight, but we arrived at my new room without any mishaps.

While the assistant got me settled into bed and my belongings unpacked, my ICU nurse gave the transfer report to my new nurse. When she finished, she came over to my bed, put something in my hand, and closed my fist.

"You need this right now more than I do. It was given to me when I needed help, and now, I'm paying it forward."

As she turned and walked out with the assistant, I opened my hand to see what she gave me. Tears filled my eyes when I realized what it was—a beautiful cross on a chain I had seen around her neck. I never saw her again, but I vowed that someday I too would repay the kindness to another person in need. I was determined to change and become a better person.

My floor nurse introduced himself as he checked all of my tubes and listened to my lungs, heart, and belly. I was so done with being in the hospital, but then I remembered Amber was still here.

I closed my eyes and tried to get some rest. The past week had taken me on a roller-coaster ride of emotions, and I was exhausted. My family tiptoed in to check on me, and I heard them say they would come back when I was awake. I would have opened my eyes to acknowledge their presence, but I wasn't quite ready to talk about what happened.

"I hope you're hungry," the nurse said as he returned with my breakfast tray. "I'll be back in a while."

I pretended to sleep so I wouldn't have to deal with reality, but the idea of staying tethered to all of the tubes and lines motivated me to start being an active participant in my healing process. The food was bland, but I was grateful for what I was given.

When my nurse returned, he seemed pleased with my progress. "I'm glad you're doing better," he said as he gave me a pain pill and capped off my IV for intermittent use. After that, he removed my catheter. To not have a pee bag hanging from my bed was a relief. "You'll get rid of the rest of the tubes later today if your x-rays this afternoon look okay."

I spent the majority of the morning and early afternoon sleeping and watching TV. My nurse had sensed my uncertainty about seeing my family and had sent them to the waiting room to get some rest.

By midafternoon, I could feel myself healing and getting stronger. The radiology tech returned to take me to get more x-rays. At least it was easier to get into the wheelchair this time, less tubes to deal with.

On our way back, I noticed a familiar person in the chapel. "Wait!" I said to the tech, causing him to jerk the wheelchair to a stop. As I peered into the dimly lit room, I could see Amber sitting in a wheelchair near the front of the room, her left leg propped out in front. The colorful rays of light streaming through the stained-glass window highlighted her bowed head.

"Please," I said to the tech. "I need to go in here for a few minutes."

"I understand," the tech said with an understanding smile. He bent over and whispered, "I'll be out here when you're ready to return to your room." He sat down on a bench outside the chapel next to a CNA who was also waiting for her patient.

"Thanks," I replied, slowly propelling myself to the front of the chapel. When I got to the point where Amber was, I locked the brakes on my wheelchair, bowed my head, and closed my eyes. Up until last week, it had been years since I'd prayed. Now, I felt compelled to do so. I was still alive for a reason; I just had to figure out what it was.

I silently thanked God for letting me live and for bringing my family back together. I asked for help with making good choices and to not waste the second chance I was given. When I was finished, I looked over at Amber. Embarrassment crept into my cheeks when I realized she had been watching me.

"Hi," I stammered. "How are you doing?"

"Good," she answered. "The doctor said I could leave the hospital later today. My grandparents aren't able to drive me back since I technically ran away from camp, so I'm just waiting for a ride. Gabe took Bo back to the camp to pack up his stuff and then he'll be back to get me. The judge is letting Bo go live with Jasmine and her family to help raise the baby."

"That's great!" I replied. I was truly glad that Bo was getting to start over. "Is your leg okay?"

"I should be able to walk after it's healed, but I'll never be able to compete in gymnastics again. How about you?" she asked with concern about the drains coming from my chest and abdomen.

"Those should be removed today, and I could go back to camp in the morning."

Amber reached over and lightly touched my hand. "There aren't enough words to say thanks. I would've died in the woods if you weren't there to rescue me."

I squeezed her hand to show my concern for her. "You have to promise me you won't try that again," I begged her as I raised her wrist, the bracelet sliding down enough to reveal the self-inflicted wounds over the car-accident scars.

"I promise," she said as her voice cracked. "I didn't think I had anything left to live for, but I was wrong." She composed herself then continued on, "You have the chance to have a family again. What are you gonna do?"

I thought for a minute then said, "I don't know. I've been so angry and lost over the years I wouldn't know where to start."

We sat in silence for a minute, gazing at each other. The emptiness and anger that once consumed me now faded into the past as I realized my future sat next to me.

Movement behind us caught us off guard. "We didn't mean to sneak up on the two of you," Trevor said as he approached us with Mom and Matt. "Do you mind if we sit with you?"

"No," I answered. "You can come in if you want to."

"Hello, Mrs. Parker," Amber said as she extended her hand to Mom.

"It's so nice to meet you," Mom replied and gently shook Amber's hand. "We were so worried about the two of you."

"Thanks," Amber said graciously, impressed there were more people than she realized who actually cared about her. "I need to get back to my room and pack before Gabe returns. I'm really sorry for causing so much trouble," she apologized to Trevor.

"Everything happens for a reason," he said with a smile. "If it weren't for your escape, I would never have been reunited with my family." Trevor gave her a light pat on the shoulder as he helped her turn her wheelchair around. "Do you want me to take you back to your room?" he asked.

"No, thanks," Amber responded. "I have a CNA waiting outside for me. Besides, I think the four of you probably have a lot of catching up to do."

As I watched her leave, an unfamiliar nervousness and anxiety shadowed my newly developed self-confidence.

Amber was my friend. She didn't care about what I had done in the past. Her faith and trust in me made me want to become a better person. *What if my family didn't see me the way that she did? What if they believed I would always remain a delinquent? I believed in my ability to change, but would they?* I was about to find out.

CHAPTER 17

Mom approached me first, tears in her eyes. She knelt down in front of me and put her hand on my knee. "Please forgive me for making the decision to send you away for the summer," she said with her words catching in her throat. "I had no other options. I didn't want you to end up in prison or, worse, dead. I couldn't deal with losing you too."

I could tell the decision had torn her up inside. Lines of guilt and worry, not to mention the recent lack of sleep, had creased her face. "I was so mad at first," I admitted to her. "I felt betrayed and alone. Now, I'm glad you made such a tough choice. Without camp, I would've never found a reason to be a better person and to stay out of trouble. I met my grandpa, a cousin, friends, and a girl who liked me for who I really am. Best of all, I realized there's so much more to life even after it ends. It's me that should be asking you for forgiveness."

"Your dad would be so proud of you," Mom said, beaming.

"I know," I said. "I met Dad twice—once while I was by the river trying to get help for Amber and then again when I was in the OR having a near-death experience."

By then, Mom had tears streaming down her face. "Did he say anything about Ian?"

"As a kid, there were a couple of times I saw Ian," I revealed. "I saw him when I was at his funeral and when I fell out of Aunt Bea's tree, but I never said anything to anyone. I figured nobody would believe me anyway."

"I believe you. It always felt like Ian was still with us, just in a different way," Mom said as she wrapped her arms around me. "I love you so much." We clung to each other, making up for years of lost time.

"I love you too," I answered, flooded with emotion. "I'm so sorry for my behavior. I've become a better person, especially since I learned about Jesus and the sacrifices he made for me. I can't wait to get home and tell you about my week."

"I'd like that," Mom said as she stood up and wiped her tear-streaked cheeks.

I quickly wiped my own face as Trevor approached. He too knelt down in front of my wheelchair to talk.

"The experience of meeting my family has been indescribable," Trevor divulged with glistening eyes. "It's like a part of TJ has been returned to me."

"I never had a grandpa before this week," I replied. "I dreamed about what it would be like to have one when I was little but never thought I would get the chance. I don't know what to call you, though."

Trevor chuckled. "You can call me whatever you like."

"How about Gramps?" I asked with a smile.

"Perfect!" he said. "It's nice to have another grandson in the family." He extended his hand to shake mine, but I surprised him with a big hug instead.

Matt was the final member in the group to visit me. He remained standing in front of me since he was a lot shorter than everyone else. Even though I had spent all week with him, it was different now. It was almost like I had a younger brother again.

"How are you doin'?" he asked with worry on his face.

"Much better than I look," I joked, which brought an immediate sigh of relief from Matt.

An impish grin formed on Matt's mouth. "Good! I would hate to be stuck with your toilet duty while you're lazin' around!"

"Ha! Ha!" I attempted a laugh until the pain in my side and middle cut it short. "I'll be back to myself in no time, and you'll wish I was still gimpy!"

"I'm glad you're okay," Matt said as he extended his hand for a fist bump.

"Me too," I said as our fists met.

"I should probably head back to my room before my nurse thinks I went AWOL," I teased my family. "I'm supposed to get discharged in the morning. If you guys want to go home and get some sleep, I'll be all right here. No attempt to escape, I promise," I quipped.

"I'm staying until you're discharged," Mom answered. "I'd rather sleep on a couch at the hospital than go back home without you."

"Besides," Trevor added with a grin, "the food here isn't that bad."

My family said their good-byes as the radiology tech came in to wheel me back to my room.

"It looks like your reunion went well," he said as he pushed the wheelchair down the hall.

"Yeah, it did. Thanks for your advice this morning. I really needed that," I said with a sincerity that comes with a true change of heart. I could definitely tell I was a different person than I was a week before.

"You're welcome," he replied. "Everyone needs to know they're loved. I'm glad you made the right choices today. It'll be the start of a whole new you."

"I appreciate that," I responded as he wheeled me into my room and helped me into bed.

"I'll let your nurse know you're back. Good luck." And with that, the radiology tech left.

By then, it was late afternoon. My nurse entered the room with a smile. "Good news," he said. "The x-rays are clear, so I'll be removing your abdominal drain. Your doctor will be in soon to remove the chest tube. Take this pain pill now, and I'll be back in a few minutes after it's kicked in."

"Thanks," I said as I took the pill.

I was glad I had the pill in me when the nurse and doctor came back in to remove my tubes. The searing pain was more intense than I had expected, but it was worth it to have them out. I still had the IV in, but the nurse said he would remove it after my last few doses of antibiotics.

The rest of the afternoon and for most of the evening, I was visited by my family. Trevor told us stories about my dad when he was a boy. Gramps said Dad was so gentle and kind to people and animals, and he was always building things with whatever materials he found around the house. Once, he had even built a tree house with multiple rooms and levels. From what I'd seen at camp, I could tell Dad had amazing talent.

I also learned the friction between my grandparents drove them apart. Grandma Charlotte just couldn't forgive Grandpa Trevor for his poor decisions. He begged her to not take the kids away and prevent them from communicating with him while he was serving time for the armed robbery. He loved them and would've done almost anything to undo what he had done. Dad was only thirteen, and Aunt Ali was eleven when Gramps was sent upstate to the prison. They never saw him again.

Mom told me how she met Dad when they were sixteen, and they instantly became high school sweethearts. He never said a word to her about Trevor other than he was dead. Also, Dad never introduced her to Charlie. Apparently, he tried to forget about his family's problems by pretending he didn't have a family.

I learned Mom always held out hope that Dad would come back. She said she would never love anyone the way she did him. I'm sure her heart broke again when she found out about Dad's accident.

Talking with Matt, I realized we were raised under similar circumstances. We both lost immediate family members in tragic accidents. The ways we chose to deal with reality, however, had been quite different. Even though I was a few years older, I felt a bond with Matt. I was glad I'd be going back to camp to spend more time with my newfound family.

My family decided it was time to leave when I could hardly stay awake during our visit. They said I needed to rest, and they wouldn't be far away. I was just drifting off to sleep when Amber stopped by my room to tell me goodbye. I could hear her awkwardly moving around with her crutches, unable to tiptoe. My eyelids felt too heavy to open as she leaned over and kissed my forehead. Quietly, she repeated the bedtime prayer I told her: "Goodnight, and may God's angels watch over you." I heard Gabe whispering to Amber it was time to return to camp. Relieved to have assurance that Amber was safe and on-the-mend, I gave into my fatigue.

That night, I had the best sleep and the most peaceful, reassuring dream I had ever experienced. I dreamed it was a warm spring day, and I was walking through a beautiful field with Amber. Excited laughter from a little voice echoed around us. Everything was perfect and as it should be.

I woke up the next morning at peace with myself, my family, and my past. It was time to look toward my future.

CHAPTER 18

The morning hospital routine was uneventful. I finished breakfast then waited for the doctor's official discharge order. It didn't take long to complete all the formalities and paperwork once he came by.

"You're lucky to be alive," the doctor told me as I was checking out at the nurses' station with my family. "Not many people can say they've died and come back."

"I had a guardian angel watching out for me," I replied with a confident smile.

"Best of luck to you," he said as he shook my hand.

"Thanks," I said as we proceeded down the hallway toward the elevator. I tried to convince the staff to let me walk to the exit, but they insisted I be taken out by wheelchair. I'm glad I didn't try to argue with them.

"Would it be all right if I rode back to camp with Mom?" I asked Trevor. "I promise I won't do anything stupid," I added with a grin.

"That would be fine with me," he replied. "I trust you."

Wow. I haven't heard that much. "Thanks," I said with relief in my voice.

I spent part of the ride back to New Beginnings Camp reflecting upon my recent experiences. It was hard to believe just one week ago, I was standing in front of Judge Mosaron being sentenced to camp. I was angry and lost. Now I was glad to be going back. I would soon see Amber, and I now had hope for a brighter future.

Except for some leaves and branches lying on the side of the highway, all indications of the storm two days before were gone. The sunlight filtering down through the trees was peaceful and inspiring. I didn't feel the nauseating, chest-tightening dread that I did the first time I was brought to camp.

"I'm sorry," I said simply to Mom.

"For what?" she asked as she steered her car along the curvy highway.

"For being such a jerk the past few years."

She glanced at me with a surprised look then returned her focus to the road ahead. "Your reactions were normal for what you'd been through," she explained. "I should've been there more for you. It was my responsibility as a mother to comfort you, and I'm sorry I failed. I was so wrapped up in my own grief I neglected to see you had just as much pain, if not more."

"I promise to try harder to be a better person before the school year starts. I want to make you proud of me."

"Honey," she said as her eyes filled with tears, "I've always been proud of you."

I reached over and put my hand on hers. The years of isolating myself and feeling like I wasn't worthy of love or forgiveness disappeared.

We continued on in silence, the kind where you don't feel any need to fill it with meaningless chatter. My mom's presence was all I needed.

When we arrived at the main gate, it was open. Trevor and Matt had just entered and were greeted by the staff and other campers. Mom pulled into a parking space at the main building and turned off the engine.

"You okay?" she asked as she helped me out of the passenger seat.

"Never better," I answered with a confidence that almost surprised me.

"Welcome back!" Junior said as he shook my hand. "We were so worried about you."

"Thanks! It's good to be back," I answered Junior.

I saw Officer Bradley descend the main stairs. He had just brought a new camper up from town to fill Bo's empty spot in our cabin. "You were right," I said with an impish grin. "The forest was brutal!"

He nodded his head and smiled. "I'll be back to take you home when your sentence is finished."

"I'll see you at the end of the summer," I said.

My friends grabbed my bag and helped me back to our cabin to unpack.

"Come with me, and I'll give you a tour of the camp," Trevor invited Mom. "TJ did an amazing job when he designed and built this place."

"I knew he was talented," Mom said, "but I had no idea he was capable of this." The sprawling campus and beautiful, majestic design of the main lodge had her speechless.

When their tour was complete, Trevor stopped by the towering cross. He motioned me over as I carefully navigated the steps of Courage cabin. It took me awhile to slowly make my way across the yard to where Trevor and Mom stood.

"I wish we could have all been reunited while TJ was alive," Trevor said, "but all things happen for a reason. Our past, present, and future are all known by God. I had this cross erected in TJ's memory. I buried his ashes at the base of the cross, and I had this plaque created for him."

In loving memory of TJ Parker, developer
of New Beginnings Camp for Troubled Youth

> May his gift of second chances be an ever-present reminder of God's grace and forgiveness.

There wasn't a dry eye between the three of us.

"Thank you, Trevor," Mom sniffled. "It's beautiful."

"You're welcome," he replied. "I have another surprise for you. The attorney that gave me the deed has been trying for years to locate you. TJ had apparently made a will when he left his lucrative job in Portland. You and Eli are listed as the primary beneficiaries for all of the life insurance, retirement, and investment accounts. They're valued in the millions, so you'll never have to worry about money again."

I grabbed Mom's arm to steady her. The news was overwhelming.

"Are you okay?" Trevor asked as he helped Mom to a nearby bench to sit.

"Stunned!" she replied, still trying to process what just happened.

"We're...rich?" I asked in disbelief.

"Yes, beyond anything you thought possible," Trevor clarified.

"Whoa!" I exclaimed as I sat next to Mom. I felt weak, but I wasn't sure whether it was the revelation of a secure financial future or if it was the recuperation process from surgery and my injuries. Probably both, I figured.

"The only stipulation is you have to pay it forward," Trevor explained. "Not everything, just enough to help others in the way that we've been helped."

"Of course," Mom answered. "I honestly believe TJ has been watching over us."

"Me too," Trevor echoed.

The bell rang, indicating it was time for lunch.

"I should get going," Mom said, "unless you need me to stay."

"I think I'll be okay," I responded. "I plan to spend the rest of the summer getting caught up in school. There are only two more years until graduation." I gave Mom a big hug then turned and headed toward the main building where Amber was waiting for me on the steps.

"He's becoming a wonderful young man. You did a great job raising him, Elizabeth," Trevor congratulated Mom.

"And you've done a great job as a mentor, pastor, and grandpa," Mom replied with a smile. She then returned to her car and climbed in, confident her initial decision to send me here was the right one.

Amber and I spent the remainder of the summer working hard to excel in our classes. We even spent the team-building time studying since we were both still healing from our physical injuries.

Our emotional and psychological wounds gradually faded, too. We began to trust people again. Amber began to communicate with the staff and develop friendships with the other campers. She continued to wear her bracelets as reminders of the pain she conquered rather than as ways to conceal it.

I became a leader in our cabin, teaching the new campers the rules and guiding them with the "been there, done that" insight. My anger and rebellion were gone, replaced by peace and the genuine desire to help others.

The last week of camp, Amber and I made the decision to become a part of Christ's family. Our wounds had healed, so Trevor baptized us with several other campers in the swimming pool. It was amazing to realize someone loved us so much that he endured death on a cross to save us from our sins. All we had to do was accept his love and sacrifice for us, and we would be his children forever. The thought of seeing both of my fathers in heaven someday was exciting.

By the final week in August, most of the campers had completed their sentences and were scheduled to leave on the same day. We were each asked to pack up our belongings in the cabins and return to the Transformation Room to collect the personal items we checked in with. I decided to throw away the piercing I used to wear in my lip. I didn't intend to repierce the area that had closed up weeks ago. Besides, the only jewelry I wore now was the cross my hospital nurse gave me. As for the clothing I came in with and the extra outfits in my locker, I asked Gabe to donate all of it to a local shelter. I planned to go shopping for some new clothes when I got home since the safari look just wasn't my style.

We said our good-byes to friends we made and the staff who guided us in our journey. Ms. Reid told me I had made the most progress of any student she had taught before, and she even referred me to the Talented and Gifted program. Junior had moisture at the corners of his eyes as he gave out hugs. He said it was dust and pollen bothering his eyes, but I knew he was just a big teddy bear at heart.

Officer Bradley arrived driving a bus to return most of us to town. Matt decided to stay with Grandpa Trevor for a few months longer while he got acquainted with his newfound family. Mason, Kalvin, Derek, and a few other boys and girls stayed behind while they continued to work toward meeting their rehabilitation goals.

The ride back to the courthouse was fairly quiet. I think we were all afraid of getting sucked back into the lifestyle that got us sent away to begin with. We each grabbed our bag and entered the courtroom. One by one, we stood in front of Judge Mosaron. Amber was called up right before me. I couldn't hear what was said, but her grandparents were escorted into the room at the end of their conversation. They all embraced while the tears fell. As they were leaving, Amber turned and looked at me, her hands forming a heart. I knew in that moment we would be forever linked.

The judge calling my name refocused my attention. I slowly approached, wondering what he would say.

"Well, young man," he began. "I've heard good reports from the staff at New Beginnings Camp. It started out rough for you, but you've managed to turn things around. I'm proud of what you've accomplished, and I'm sure your family is as well. I expect this will be the last appearance for you in my courtroom."

"Yes, sir," I politely responded.

"Very good," he stated. "You may go."

Mom was waiting for me at the exit. We hugged then continued down the hall toward the parking lot. I briefly stopped in the entry to wipe my eyes. I told Mom I had an "eyelash" bothering me, but I'm sure she knew I was covering for the relief and emotions seeping out.

Something hanging on the wall caught my attention. As I got closer, I could tell it was a newspaper memorial that had been framed. It described the life and career of a local man named Abraham who had passed away several years before. Not only was he in law enforcement, but he was also an advocate for young people. There was something familiar about the picture. The man had weathered skin, gray hair, and a twinkle in his eye just like Judge Mosaron.

I looked at Mom, and she looked at me. "That's not him, is it?" I asked her.

"No, it couldn't be," she answered with a perplexed look. "Maybe it's a family member."

"Yeah, maybe," I said.

We left the building, never to return to it again. Mom quit her two jobs, bought a nice house just outside of town with her inheritance, and helped Trevor carry on the mission that TJ started. She never remarried, said true love comes around only once in a lifetime.

I was fortunate to have been given such a life-changing opportunity to learn from my mistakes and grow from them. Most of the campers I met changed as well. Carter and Zack overcame their fears and became standout athletes on their equestrian and swim teams. Kalvin traveled the country as a motivational speaker. Bo married Jasmine, and they became wonderful parents to Kenzie. Eddie went on to MIT, graduated at the top of his class, and started one of the most successful software companies in the nation. Max moved back home after realizing how lucky he was to have a family.

Not everyone was as fortunate, though. Vaughn and Derek let their anger define who they were. After they finally completed the program at camp, they returned to the same lifestyle and ended up in prison for murder and manslaughter. They are still incarcerated.

Although Mason completed the program and never did drugs again, the damage he had done to his body was more than it could handle. He died from cardiac arrest at just twenty-one years of age.

Matt stayed at camp with Grandpa Trevor for a few more months after I was released then was encouraged to move in with Mom and me. Trevor said he wanted him to have a more normal upbringing than be constantly surrounded by troubled kids.

We still saw Gramps on a weekly basis. Mom learned how to manage the camp and eventually took over when Trevor was ready to retire. She said she needed to do something to help people. It was who she was.

I found out at the beginning of that first school year back that Amber transferred to the same high school as me. From the moment we were reunited, we were inseparable. We were in the same classes and went to the same church. When we were apart, it was as if a part of me was missing.

The spark that began at New Beginnings Camp for Troubled Youth grew into an eternal love. After graduating from college, we got married.

Amber earned her degrees in education and business prior to opening her own gym. She teaches gymnastics to children and had several former students make the Olympic team. Her once severely injured leg healed to near-perfect condition, although the occasional twinge reminds her of our fateful weekend so long ago.

I went on to medical school and became a pediatrician. It was the most challenging—yet rewarding—of all career paths I could have chosen. Every so often, I find myself smiling, knowing that Dad and Ian are looking down on me. I believe when I see them again, they'll give me a hug and tell me how pleased they are with my transformation and accomplishments.

As I stand here now, I am amazed by the gifts God has given me. I watch Amber dancing through the tall meadow grass speckled with wildflowers, her auburn hair gleaming in the sunlight, and her rounded abdomen revealing that our precious little girl will soon arrive. The cross necklace I gave her when our sentences at camp were complete sparkles against her ivory skin. I hear our young son giggling as he chases after her, trying to catch the butterflies gliding through the air. In the distance, the beautiful song of the finches in the trees floats upon the warm, gentle breeze. I reflect back upon all that has occurred since that fateful week years ago, and I realize everything is perfect and as it should be.

ABOUT THE AUTHOR

I was born, raised, and educated in the beautiful state of Oregon, where I continue to live with my husband and our two children. I've been a registered nurse since 1997 and have worked in a variety of settings and specialties. Providing care to patients from different types of backgrounds has helped shape who I am—patient, kind, optimistic, and dedicated.

Beyond Ikenick Creek was initially written to encourage my children to read more. During the literary journey, it became an opportunity to reach out to people searching for meaning and purpose. Encouraging people, especially the youth, to make good choices is an investment in the future. Teaching them about Christianity is an investment in their eternity.

For more information, please visit my website at www.traceymayfield.com.